S0-BFI-323

Evening Sessions with Dr Priestly

Evening Sessions with Dr Priestly

A testament to psychoanalysis

by Cathy Lobel

Copyright ©2007 by Cathy Lobel
All rights reserved. Published by Two Lights Press

www.EveningSessions.com
cathylobel@rcn.com

ISBN 13: 978-0-615-17095-4

Excerpt from "Rowing" from THE AWFUL ROWING TOWARD GOD by Anne Sexton.
Copyright © 1975 by Loring Conant, Jr.,Executor of the Estate of Anne Sexton.
Used by permission of Houghton Mifflin Company. All rights reserved.

Library of Congress Cataloging-in-Publication Data tk

Printed in the United States of America
Manufactured by Edwards Brothers, Ann Arbor, MI

Cover art & design: Austin + Chris Metze, www.metzedesign.com

Contents

Let my people go that they may make a feast unto me in the wilderness
—Exodus

The message of psychoanalysis—four words: go dream world feast

Introduction

This book—written from a patient's perspective—attempts to describe what can happen in psychoanalysis: how one can grow and change in unexpected ways and how creativity can emerge from the unconscious mind, where beauty and linguistic exuberance flourish.

Being in psychoanalysis is surprisingly akin to religious experience. Both call on faith. Both offer hope. In both, we may seek protection, communion, release—we seek the promise of blessings. To my way of thinking, psychoanalysis is a blessing.

In treatment, patients hearken to the analyst's message, which is as old as *Genesis* itself: *Go forth—and journey to the land that I will show you.* And by hearkening, patients journey home to the land of the self— that vital and undiscovered country. In the process, they learn what often proves to be a new and foreign language: the prickly language of the heart. This is the language spoken in psychoanalysis and the role of the analyst is to help restore patients to the heart of themselves. The role of the analyst is to help allow the patient to develop her own nurturing inner mother—to allow the patient to incorporate the analyst's goodness and compassion into herself, forever, so that the patient will not be at a loss living her life. She will know what to do with her life. And because the analyst's goodness is so vital to the process, it is absolutely essential that the analyst be a good analyst.

When I entered treatment, I had no idea what psychoanalysis was or how it worked. I trusted no one, least of all a so-called healer. But I knew right away that I'd more than met my match in Dr Priestly. And it was her interest in me, her active pursuit of what was going on inside me (inside? I really had an inside?), that meant to me I was sufficiently worthy—sufficient despite my impoverished beginnings and unabated outbursts. I could put my rage and pain, all my sorrows, into the hands of this devoted being. She would help me start anew—resuscitate me, raise me up, even at this late date—to become a happier, livelier person, and to recover untapped gifts apparently overlooked before.

It must be said that I was no light lunch. I was a complicated oddball—and it would take years of evening sessions to even me out. I was constantly up in arms, resisting her, refusing to look in the mirror, hating to look at myself. I didn't want to see. Contemptuous and stuck, cut off from the goodness inside, I didn't want her to interpret anything painful or frightening. I wanted her to just shut up. But she didn't shut up.

It was clear that I hadn't been raised up right (I'd hardly been raised up at all). I didn't know how to talk. Suspicion colored my perception. I lacked social grace and moral compass. I didn't even know what religion I was until I was eight and it cannot truly be said that I've found religion since.

I had no dream, no dreams. In my entire life before treatment, I could count on five fingers all the dreams I'd ever remembered. But under pressure from Dr Priestly, I promptly began remembering them, much to my amazement.

Not only at the outset but through nearly the full course of treatment I had read virtually nothing in the bible. Yet, the dreams I brought Dr Priestly often invoked religious imagery. I dreamt of Moses on the Mount, of dancing with Christ, of stigmata—in visceral ways that nearly took my breath away. But it wasn't until late in treatment that the question arose in my mind: where did these religious images come from?

One conclusion was that psychoanalysis and the bible tell the same story: the story of human development. Looking back, it seems a natural part of the treatment process—working on the formation of the self, the development of the child within, birth, rebirth, the growth of the moral and spirited self— that spiritual metaphors might spontaneously occur.

While everyone knows that the interpretation of dreams is central to psychoanalysis, the role of dreams and visions in the bible is arguably just as important. In fact, it might be said that the bible itself is one long dream. Perhaps we are all dreaming about the bible without realizing it.

Thinking makes me nervous. So on the infrequent occasions that I do it, I do it slowly. But the more I thought about the dreams I'd had in treatment, the more it seemed that psychoanalysis parallels the story of Exodus: hard-hearted Pharaoh stands for the "bad mother," a bully man-in-a-skirt, he's an indecipherable Egyptian sphinx mother; while Moses is the remote father as well as the midwife of the children (in a sense, he's akin not only to the psychoanalyst but also the *transforming* patient who learns how to bear the child within herself). And the children, the children of Israel, are the understandably resistant patients—impatient, recalcitrant, skeptical, backsliding, confused, and exhausted from the birth pangs of Passover and forty years of wilderness wandering, striving to be released from inner bondage and borne into a better life, craving to reach the promised land of love.

Carl Jung noted "the peculiar fact that the dream is the divine voice and messenger and yet an unending source of trouble." I couldn't have agreed more about the trouble. I constantly fled from my dreams. I constantly felt betrayed by them—sizzled and fried in their saucy reduction. In the beginning, they'd seemed like thunder bolting into me from somewhere outside. But later, I determined that, behind my back, Dr Priestly had formed a rather special relationship (a covenant?) with my dreams. Together, they were having some kind of fling, an outrageous affair during which she snuck in through the back door of my head and somehow turned them on. And then somehow those wanton dreams took me by the hand like a mother—a wild and ruthless mother who rattled me up and flung me around like a rag doll baby (all of which was approximately my sense of how, in actuality, my own mother had behaved and treated me during my childhood)

Of course one could surmise that the religious imagery in my dreams was due to the strong impact of my particular analyst, Dr Priestly, whose name so aptly befits her. I believe that my dream imagery was, at least in part, a result of my susceptibility to her influence, to the influence of her consulting room with its sacred paintings of Christs and Madonnas, and to my catching what she **un**consciously transmitted. In this sense, I feel that my dreams were *our* dreams, a kind of transporting duet between patient and analyst—a series of riffs and tiffs and love songs and catches.

Still, despite my lack of religious upbringing and despite the fact that I am not a believer in normative religions, it seems I entered treatment strongly predisposed to the grandeur of religious imagery. It was from the outset that I brought Dr Priestly dreams filled with such imagery. And throughout my years of evening sessions, I struggled to be' blessed' by her. I fought tooth and nail, I fought like Jacob with his Angel, to wrest, wrangle, extract, or otherwise elicit (all quite unsuccessfully) from her the title of most wonderful patient, a chosen one. More accurately, I fought tooth and nail to become true to myself. I longed to be as true to myself as I felt she was to herself, as full of spirit in the best sense—to possess what struck me as her brand of generosity of spirit, her warmth and wisdom and hospitality, her unconventionality, her brave soul. I suppose that in the playhouse of my imagination I dreamt that she stood for—I **needed** her to stand in for—a cavalcade of living myths, of culture heroes who I could look up to the way a child looks up to tall tales, godlike parents. I think I felt that if she could stand for all this, then I—in the shadow of her wings—I, by association, would be the recipient of such powerful and beneficent grand standing.

And so she stood. She stood for my varied notions of heroism even as she withstood my idealizations, balking and bashing. And all the while, she stood by me helping me to resurrect myself. She stood up for me, for the lost parts—the thwarted parts—of me. She had an enduring faith—not only in her own ability to teach but also in her patients' capacity to respond.

For me, coming of age in psychoanalysis, Dr Priestly was my midwife, my poet of riddles, my rabbi. Of course, one's unconscious mind "does its thing." Its inner force is incredibly powerful—as powerful as a god— and perhaps more potent than any relationship. But I couldn't have done the work on myself alone. It was Dr Priestly's fierce insight and unrelenting insistence that helped compel me to face reality. Both stranger and angel—paradoxically elliptical and confronting, tormenting and uplifting, she delivered to me the message of what it means to be human, what it means to join with others in the human community.

Near the end of treatment, as the trance of treatment was ending, when at long last I started wondering where the biblical imagery in my dreams came from, I began reading small portions of the bible and was utterly startled by how many of its elements, previously unknown to me, seemed to mirror my dreams. And it was then that I read that most fascinating book, **The Book of J**, in which the literary critic Harold Bloom had this to say about the bible's first author, the J writer:

"In Jerusalem, nearly three thousand years ago, an unknown author composed a work that has formed the spiritual consciousness of much of the world ever since. We possess only a fragmentary text of that work, embedded within what we call Genesis, Exodus, and Numbers.... My assumption is that J (the J writer) was...an immensely sophisticated, highly placed member of the Solomonic elite, enlightened and ironic. My primary surmise is that J was a woman (and) essentially a comic writer....It is one of the multitude of extraordinary ironies concerning J that this author upon whom Western religious moralism ultimately must rely is herself the least moralistic of writers."

How very thrilling—because if the author of the bible is a woman, maybe God, if there is a God, is a woman. And all of this is to say that the deepest strand of the bible was written by an artist.

And reading **The Book of J,** I felt that the J writer and Dr Priestly had certain qualities in common: nobility, elliptical irony, originality and artistry. And later, as I began reading about Jesus of Nazareth who, as Harold Bloom put it, was "a poet of riddles," I could see that he was an extraordinary artist, a fiercely here-and-now teacher and healer, a rabbi whose words are fire. And this too reminded me of Dr Priestly.

As I thought more about it, I could see that the J writer and Jesus of Nazareth had something very much in common: an unflinching capacity to show us who we are. To hold up the mirror to ourselves and say: Look, now look.

And this also is a quality Dr Priestly possesses. The capacity of a warm and gifted human being, a psychoanalyst who can't stop helping save her patients—by seeing who they are and by imaginatively conceiving who they have the capacity to become—by helping them dream of coming to life, of being pregnant with life, helping them struggle against the threat of a miscarried life.

Preface on Structure, Illustrations & Sources

Each set of left-and-right-hand facing pages (each spread) in this book is intended as a unit—with the left hand page referring to something scriptural and universal, and the right hand referring to the specific experience of my psychoanalysis. One might say the left functions as a kind of Greek Chorus in relation to the right. And perhaps the right—while presenting a highly personal portrait, occasionally acts as commentary, as midrash, in relation to the left.

The visual images that punctuate the text are miniature perhaps because they represent the long ago faraway world-in-little of childhood. This seems only fitting since much of psychoanalysis involves the child within the self, a "shrinking back" in one's head, to the child inside. And too, much of our religious heritage springs from the childhood of humanity.

At the same time, something in these tiny images feels to me like a strange cross between the miniature pictures found in medieval **Books of Hours** and the illustrated poetry of **archy and mehitabel**—archy being the dung beetle-ish creature who processes words with his entire body but who's so small he can barely stretch far enough to type in upper case or use punctuation— and mehitabel, the alley cat who claims to have been Cleopatra in a former life.

The dreams presented (chronologically) in my text occasionally appear in hexameter. Although I obviously don't dream in hexameter, I confess to having previously experienced most of my dreams as a **hex**. Having learned to better tolerate them over the years, I've subsequently re-written most of them in prose.

My biblical sources are of a magpie variety: among them are **The Book of J** by Harold Bloom with David Rosenberg's translation; William Tyndale's translation of the **New Testament** (Worms edition of 1526 in original spelling, The British Library)**;** the Soncino edition of **The Pentateuch;** and the text of the **Gospel of Thomas (The Complete Gospels: Annotated Scholar's Version)**.

A complete list of sources, biblical and otherwise, appears at the end of this book.

Part 1

Parenthetical Love

(You're driving me buggy)

:

In the Beginning

In the beginning, the earth was chaos and void
And darkness was on the face of the deep

And the spirit of God hovered on the face of the water.

—Genesis 1: 1-2

Right from the beginning, Dr Priestly drove me buggy. Hovering, pressing me forward, setting limits left and right, speaking in a language that was totally new.

She was always throwing her weight around, always trying to pin me down. On the one hand, I wanted to be pinned to her. But on the other hand, I didn't want to be stuck by her.

She infuriated me—acting like a Sphinx or Moses on the Mount. Who did she think she was? That indecipherable bitch

But in time, I came to adore her. I felt held in her (parenthetical) embrace, her parental embrace. And I concluded that psychoanalysis is (parenthetical) love.

A land of milk and honey

 Pharaoh said to the children of Israel:
Every son that is born ye shall cast into the river.

So the infant Moses got put in an ark of bulrushes and laid by the river's brink

Pharaoh's daughter found him there and adopted him into her royal family

Later, God promised Moses:
I will bring you up out of Egypt, land of affliction, across the Sea, and unto a land flowing with milk and honey

—Exodus 1:22; 2:3, 10; 3:8

A plague of fees

I concluded that psychoanalysis is much more than a plague of fees.

Not raised up right, how else—but under the direction of Dr Priestly—could I be contained in a secure hold? How else could I reach the promised land of love?

Since in the beginning I was a basket case < > I needed guidance and protection.

So that was why she was always lording over me—carrying on about how recalcitrant I was and what a spineless pile of mush I was. How all I wanted was to be taken care of. All I wanted was a lullaby.

But one thing I knew for sure: If she fucking cared so much about me, she should adopt me.

And another thing: there was simply no way, NO WAY, for me to start out reclining on the couch facing up. I'd be too lost at sea, I'd have been drowned.

< >

No. I didn't get put on the couch until I had my crazy canoe dream.

My crazy canoe dream

A canoe glides across the pupil of her eye
as the girl pumps up much too high on a playground swing.
She ends up falling down, down, down; lands with an awful
THUD—oh god—right next to an ancient stone marker
and an Egyptian stone cat half-buried in sand.

What that dream meant who knew? The rush and gravity of it was terrifying. My eye would be cut, slit open. Torn apart, I was being torn apart. I'd already been torn apart and the truth of that revelation was blinding. I would be thrown—or pulled—down, I'd fall down, down in darkness, in abysmal failure. Please stay with me, Dr Priestly. Hold me please. Don't leave me.

It took me forever to catch what I later thought was my dream's pun—its speech impediment—to catch its underhanded way of seeking help from my analyst:

Canoe (can you) teach me to be the pupil of my eye (the student of my I)?

Can you save me from drowning? < > Can you rescue me from ruin?

Meanwhile, Dr Priestly didn't explain in words what my dream meant. Just as I didn't put my fear in words

She assigned me then and there to recline on the couch, under her direction. Meaning I'm to be so totally exposed? Flat on my back—my breasts, my belly exposed—where she can see me but I can't see her? Facing up in the evening light?

And even though I longed to just let go, this made my teeth chatter.

But they constrained him, saying:
Abide with us; for it is toward evening, and the day is far spent.
--Luke 24:29

And Jesus said:
Be not afraid. I am with you, always, even unto the end of time
—Matthew 28:10, 20

When love was murder

Yes.
 And thinking back to those early days also reminded me how in session
sometimes the perspiration used to drip down the nape of my neck. A long time
ago, Dr Priestly put her hand on my neck and I realized she was doing it to see how perspiry
and anxious I was. I mean, in the very beginning I had been so anxious, so terrified. I don't
mean now—I don't mean now that I'm going onto the couch. I mean before.

Before—when it really felt like holy hell in here—in her consulting room

I mean in the beginning when I thought I could be murdered alive.
When I thought love was murder

I mean when all I could think was for her to please stay with me. Hold me please. Don't leave
me. When I was trembling but I didn't know how to tell her. But she knew.

And now I think it's time—it's really time—for me to lie down.
Now I lay me down on her couch

Like a bridge over troubled water
I will lay me down

And God said to Moses:
Now go. I will be thy mouth and teach thee what to speak.
—Exodus 4:12

You'll teach me how to talk?

The canoe dream wasn't the first dream I'd brought Dr Priestly. I'd brought plenty of dreams before that—because she said I **had** to bring dreams

Right from the beginning, I tried to bring her the kind of dream I thought she'd appreciate:

*Moses—Wisdom—stands in a world that's **upside-down**.*
A trembling world, full of earthquakes, rent in chaos

I stand below—looking up at (up to?) Moses— 👤👤 *who's very*

High on a Peak that looks like an upside-down **V:** ▲

But no matter what little dream gifts I brought to placate her, Dr Priestly proved about as predictable as a volcano.

She'd start out asking my feelings about my dreams and of course I'd say that was *her* job to figure out. Then I'd tell her a thing or two. Like when she asked about the Moses dream, I said: the world *is* upside-down and Moses was remote and withdrawn, like daddy. Moses got somehow juggled into a position of leadership, like me. But really, he was an outsider, an orphan. My mummy was an orphan

And then I'd slump in my chair and she'd ask if I needed a pillow to sit up properly. Then she'd tell me *I* was the one who was **upside-down**. That *mine* was a ridiculous omnipotence.

Fuck her. She can stick it up her ass, I told her.

She said she'd have to teach me how to talk.

But who am I that I should go to Pharaoh?
Who am I to bring forth the children?
Moses asked

   —Exodus 3:11

Wait a minute—this is heady stuff...

Wait a minute—she's supposed to be raising me up—not putting me down. She shouldn't call me upside-down. This is not good. She shouldn't say such cruel and heartless things. She should just shut up.

But she proceeds to tell me that as a young child I'd had more responsibility than I could manage. She says my mother had the idea I was to be in charge of my baby brother. I was to raise him up. I should oversee him? But how could I do that—I was so little and he was such a big-headed baby to tote that whenever I tried to cart him around, *I* ended up looking **up** at **him**

When I pulled him from his baby buggy, I feared I'd drop him. I was unable to bear him. He was too heavy for me. And how could I stay planted on the ground pulling his weight and meantime navigate the shifting sands of mother's crazy mixed-up instructions? I couldn't bear her carrying on—Do this! Do that! As though I was her little slave

Dr Priestly said I **was** a slave. Compliant, she said. She has some nerve saying that. Didn't she say mother wanted *me* to be in charge, head of the household? Dr Priestly is supposed to make me feel special, like a chosen one. So what's she doing implying I'm a baby—a baby who needs a pillow to prop up right?

Because if that's what she's thinking, good by. Let me out of here. CUT. This is starting to give me as big a headache as the one I grew up with. Is she telling me she'll baby sit with me while I have to go through this stuff all over again?

Lonely fighter, Dr Priestly interrupted me to say. But wait a minute, I say—I'm still confused about my dream of Moses: I'd thought Dr Priestly was Moses in the dream. But are the two figures—Moses and me—supposed to be two aspects of myself—my self divided?—an omnipotent part and a puny little terrified part?

In my house somebody had to keep a head, right? Somebody had to keep a lid on things. And that somebody was me. And that's why the frightened, mushy, unbearable stuff in me never came out, it got stuck, it didn't get born—while the rest of me buzzed ahead, the rest of me persevered

The sea of maternal embrace?

I couldn't stand a lot of what Dr Priestly had to say. I mean, she said **she'd** have to teach **me** how to talk but meanwhile I never met anybody who could be so rude and prickly.

She's relentless—always provoking me—trying to get a rise out of me—hurling things in my face the way mother used to hurl plates around the kitchen. Telling me I'm **so** passive, **so** evasive, **so** dependent, **so** power hungry, **so** afraid to step into the unknown—telling me I have no center, I'm tossed around on an ocean. **So** what

And as for the dreams I was having to put up with, it took me a long time to notice they were full of puns and spells.

Sometimes they even behaved like spelling bees ●with their letters dancing upside down and so forth, like the **M** and **W** in the dream with Moses. Other times they had numbers. I guess it'd be fair to say they *got* my number.
☐
They made me taut all right—they practically laid me low with their crazy spelling lessens. The whole of psychoanalysis is just like that—a spell, a trance—

Here I'd be trying to comply with Dr Priestly, speaking of Moses and Mount Sinai, Peak of Peaks, saying how highly I thought of her when suddenly behind my back she'd slip the dream's message right out from under my feet and throw me into a mounting rage

Then she'd start making proclamations left and right that got me so piqued I'd want to knock her off that high horse of hers. I'd want to drown her out or fling her into the sea. The sea of maternal embrace, she would say. Does maternal embrace mean I'm a baby child? Is that what all this means? I'm supposed to allow myself to feel helpless and weak?

I'll only do it if she holds me.

And God said to Moses: Stretch out your hand over the Sea so the waters drown the Egyptians and their chariots

And the waters covered the chariots and horsemen and all the host of Pharaoh that came into the Sea after them.

But the children of Israel walked on dry land in the midst of the Sea.

Thus God saved the children that day out of the hand of the Egyptians.

Then Moses and the children sang a song unto the Lord:

> The horse and his rider hath
> He thrown into the sea

—Exodus 14:16-30; 15:1

Lying on the Couch

Once I started lying on the couch, the consulting room suddenly looked different. I started noticing things I hadn't seen before.

High up on top of a bookcase is
a bronze horse-drawn ancient warrior in a little chariot.
Is he Egyptian…or Roman?

He has a spear in hand.   en garde

I asked Dr Priestly if he'd throw his spear down at me.

She said he's harmless.

I recall asking her long ago how to get over the rage of my past, how not to drown in withdrawal.

She'd said she'd show me how.

And at the end of *that* session she'd stretched out her hand toward me—she took my hand, held my hand and led me toward the door. At that moment I knew she was good and I felt that maybe—sometimes—what is real is good.

Who is like unto thee, O Lord?

The Lord is...strength and song. The Lord is a man of war.
Thou didst blow with thy wind, the sea covered the Egyptians: they sank as lead.
The depths have covered them: they sank into the bottom as a stone.

—Exodus 15: 2, 3, 11

Are you my mother?

But what was real really wasn't so good. A lot of my past life really hadn't been too good and mostly I wanted to get away—as far away from it as possible—away from my past, away from my mother. I wanted to lead a better life than hers had been.

I wanted to wring out her venom, expunge the evidence of her
The same way I'd expunged the evidence of my own neediness—the same way I swallowed my own baby teeth—like seed pearls lost in a sea of shit.

The teeth of the evidence ● Like little loose pebbles in my rattled up head ●

All my life I felt I'd been kicked in the teeth, or kicked out. Dr Priestly said I felt I'd been kicked out.

So I learned how to beat everybody to the punch. That was my best defense. I had big muscles in my arms to prove it, I showed them to Dr Priestly one day I showed how I could puff myself up. But other times, I felt like that lost stubby-winged bird that fell out of the nest in the children's book, **Are You My Mother?** Still, mostly I fended off the world by attacking myself before anybody else could get me.

I knew I'd been dropped. From the time I was a baby flailing around in the mess and stench of the changing table or else on-all-4s squirming around in the dark, I knew I'd been dropped because I was bad. It was my fault I'd been dropped. So just shut up and don't say anything more about it. Let's just get on with it

And as for my dreams, they scared the living daylights out of me. *That's* why I didn't want to remember them. I wanted to drop them just like my mother dropped me. Cut and run

But Dr Priestly told me she liked my anger. She said it was reality-oriented.

Moses the Egyptian?

$\mathcal{S}$igmund Freud, founder of psychoanalysis, made a few wild speculations in his day. In one of his more speculative books, **Moses and Monotheism,** he had this to say:

"In the case of Moses…it is the *second* family… (the *noble* family) by which the hero is adopted… that is his *real* one. (And) if we have the courage to accept this…then we suddenly see our way clear:

Moses is an Egyptian—probably of noble origin—whom the myth undertakes to transform into a Jew….Moses is an Egyptian whom a people needed to make into a Jew.

Another trait imputed to Moses deserves our special interest. He was said to have been 'slow of speech'—that is to say, he must have had a speech impediment so that he had to call (on his brother) for assistance…This may, in a slightly distorted way, recall the fact that Moses spoke another language and was not able to communicate without the help of his interpreter."

A psychoanalyst who's not Jewish?

Well I'm glad Dr Priestly likes my anger because sure as hell nobody else around here does. But then, she's a little unusual, you might say. Hopefully she won't turn out to be *too* unusual   because she's the one I'm counting on

I mean, she's a foreigner. She's an outsider. And very old-fashioned in her way—she's one of those old-world European émigrés from another time and place. She doesn't exactly get with the program here—here in her 'adopted' homeland. I mean she doesn't fit in even though her English is awfully good, maybe better than mine

I'm chuckling to myself, thinking back to the beginning when I wanted to spit out the awful ideas she tried to stick down my throat. She got me so upset that I jumped up and fled from her consulting room, making a beeline for the nearest bar, where I spent the night drowning my fears getting stoned out of my mind on two White Russians.

Then I went home and threw them up.

It was only much later I learned **she** was White Russian. White Russian but born somewhere or other in Europe   An outsider even where she was born   I'm still not so sure what her accent is—Russian or whatever   I haven't even figured out what White Russian is, whether it has something to do with Russian nobility or Tolstoy or what.

And at some point I finally figured out she wasn't Jewish
Whoever heard of a psychoanalyst not being Jewish?

Jacob's dream

Rebecca told Jacob: Now therefore my son, arise and flee.
And so Jacob went out from Beersheba.

And he lighted on a certain place and tarried there all night.
He took a stone of that place and put it for his pillow and lay down to sleep.

He dreamed—and behold—the Lord said:
I am your grandfather's God. The land on which you lie, to you will I give it.
Know that I am with you and will keep you wherever you go

When Jacob awaked he said: Surely the Lord is in this place and I knew it not.
And he was afraid, and said: How dreadful is this place!

Then he took the stone he'd put for his pillow and set it for a pillar
to mark the place. He called it Beth El, God's house.

Later, Jacob had to wrestle with a stranger until daybreak.

The stranger said: Let me go, for the day breaks.
Jacob said: I will not let go, unless you bless me.
Now this is the story of Jacob the patriarch—whose name was changed to Israel,
which means: the one who fights with God

—Genesis 27:43; 28:11-19; 32: 24, 26

As indecipherable as my mother

Whenever I finish telling Dr Priestly my dreams, I stick them in a shoebox. And that's the end of them. Good riddance to bad rubbish.

Who needs dreams slamming into me in the night, canoes lurching into stone markers? I'm thinking back to when that awful nightmare woke me up, I was in blinding pain, my eyes swiveling in my head, my whole body throbbing:

> *A canoe glides across the pupil of her eye*
> *as the girl pumps up much too high on a playground swing.*
> *She ends up falling down, down, down; lands with an awful*
> *THUD—oh god—right next to an ancient stone marker*
> *and an Egyptian stone cat half-buried in sand.*

Bewildering—and as indecipherable as my mother

I think dreams are fucking little upstart messages that come from god knows where and they can just damn well go back where they came from. Like Assignments from hell— I've had enough of them. I'm sick of them making an Ass of me, of being stuck between a rock and a hard place wrestling with an Analyst who forces me to struggle, who sits there all night on her Ass her royal Highness picking fights with me and putting me in pin-holds

She told me long ago: Aren't you adorable! You want to fight me.
Yes because I'm sick and tired of waiting for signs of wonder

Much later, she mused that my dream's Egyptian stone cat was a Sphinx. So I searched out the riddle, the question the Sphinx poses, which is: What is man? Or, put another way: Who am I? But I didn't stop to consider any answers to such questions. I was much too busy ruthlessly pursuing my conviction that if I obliged and performed well, I could become Dr Priestly's chosen one.

BUT

I didn't want to oblige and perform well. I'm NOT a slave. Besides which, Dr Priestly herself told me to stop performing. She said: there's nothing to prove. So then, I don't have to *DO* anything. I just have to *BE* different. I just *have* to.

And as far as Assignments go, my personal rule of thumb is: I can't tolerate them unless I'm the one doling them out. Just do what I tell you. Do what I say.

That's why, when I was little, I liked Safety Patrol. I got to wear a special badge over my Girl Scout uniform.

I could order my brother all over the courtyard in Nazi-style military formation drills. And at night, I could arm-wrestle the little twink on the bare floor trying to trap *him* in pin-holds.

I even invented the TNT club in our basement closet under the stairs. I lit the place up with candles and I wielded a hammer to bang out justice among the rabble neighbor children whose memberships I'd conscripted. I was in charge so they had to listen to ME. They had to pay dues and sometimes even hand over their little dimes in exchange for my bigger nickels.

I doled out plenty of Assignments—plenty of book reports on titles from my private lending library, like **Harriet the Spy** and **Penrod.** And I charged a tidy little sum for the privilege of borrowing those books.

Dr Priestly teased me about whether my inclination was as Editor or Terrorist (maybe she meant a small Hitler, a blind not-see?) which I really didn't think was so funny since she herself wasn't exactly a bargain when it came to being told what to do.

A gift

Jacob was greatly afraid and distressed.
Deliver me—I pray thee—from the hand of my brother, for I fear him.

He stayed there that night and took what was at hand

—as a gift—

to melt his brother Esau's heart

Then Esau embraced him, fell on his neck with kisses, weeping

Jacob said: I pray you—take my gift, my blessing brought to you

—Genesis 33: 1-11

By hook or by crook

By hook or by crook I'll win over Dr Priestly. If need be, I'll win her with my charming gifts. Because if only she'll love me, everything will be fine

I'll win her with gifts like the wrought iron cheese cutter that—when I'd first obtained it seemed so charmingly handmade 𝄢 but then—when I went to bring it to her, warily under my arm—somehow started looking alarmingly like a machete, a murderous cutlass 𝄢 And she couldn't just say thanks like polite normal people. No, she had to ask why—why did I bring this gift

And her question disarmed me, it made me feel stung or stained—as if I were bribing her or maybe she thought I had blood on my hands. Not that she said that—she didn't. But right then I remembered how once she'd said—in remarking how I used anger to come alive—that I might even smash *her*

(And how once she'd said I was quite a specimen. How once she'd said in the bosom of my family, there was no bosom)

And recalling those thoughts got me stuck—I couldn't find the way—or the words—to tell her I was desperately trying to preserve the nurturing things she was giving me, even though sometimes I wanted to wring her neck to make her shut up.

I wanted to say I didn't really spit out *all* the milk of human kindness she gave me. I wasn't *totally* upside-down. I knew what she was giving me was truly a gift. And I, in turn, wanted to reciprocate. The cheese cutter was my—I know it was clumsy—my way to partake of the preserved milk, and to cut a piece for her.

The Holy of Holies

And Jacob said: Surely the Lord is in this place and I knew it not. It must be God's house. It is the gate to heaven. It is the Holy of Holies.
—Genesis 28:17

Later, God said to Moses: Ascend. Come up to me, to the mountain. I'll give you the tablets I've written for instruction. Make me an offering. Make me a Sanctuary—a Tabernacle—and there will I meet with you. Hang a cloth partition, a veil —and bring the ark of the Testimony behind the partition .The partition will be a boundary to divide the Sanctuary from the Holy of Holies   —Exodus 24:12, 26:31-34

The tablets were God's work—the writing was God's writing. God told Moses: Write down these commandments. In accordance with them, I make a covenant with you and with Israel   —Exodus 32:16, 34:27

[   ]

Dr Priestly's Bedroom

I dread telling Dr Priestly my dream of being in her bedroom, the Holy of Holies.
She'll say I'm intrusive and that I don't respect boundaries. I myself can't bear to speak out loud of the comfort of this entrancing dream of a room—this nursery womb—where I long to hide out forever. I don't want to go out in the world. I'm scared shitless of reality. But I know in reality she wants me to be born into life. I know she's behind my pressing forward. And I don't like it.

So maybe this dream is my way of seeing into *her* private world. I mean *she's* always probing into *me*, sneaking in through the back door of my head. So then I can do that to her, too. And if she thinks she can just chase me out, this will be my way of taking her back in me:

I dream I'm climbing up the stairs to Dr Priestly's bedroom where I find a loving letter from a child who's learning to write its grandfather—but in reality, the note is inscribed in Dr Priestly's handwriting. It's as though she helped guide the child's hand in writing it. The inscription, written out 3 times, says 'I like you. I like you. I like you.' Next to the text are 3 antique stick pins filled with sparkling gems. On a table are instructions about the light. And hanging curtain-like in Dr Priestly's doorway is a gauze linen sheet, a scrim that divides the bedroom from a rooftop open court.

Somehow, although the dream's sparkly stick pins are charming, they're also dangerous, like pointy little hatpins. Like sharp, edgy needles—like me. It's not easy to admit I'm sharp—sharp and prickly. But truthfully, it's even harder to say out loud that maybe I could be a gem, a fine person. Is such an idea even remotely conceivable?

This dream is tiring me out. I need to rest in a quiet sanctuary with Dr Priestly, my dream mother, my inner mother, just the 2 of us, just our little dyad. But somehow the 2 of us is becoming 3. Everything lately and everything in the dream is in 3s—and baby makes 3? 3 is a series; a trinity, a crowd. Can I bear to cope with 3? I just want to crawl in bed and sleep. I'm exhausted

And God said to Moses:

How long will this people provoke me? How long will it be before they believe me, for all the signs which I have shown them? —Numbers 14:11

And Moses said to God:

Did I conceive this people? Did I give birth to them, so that you should say to me 'Hold them to your bosom, as a nurse carries a baby, until you arrive at the land which I vowed to your fathers?'

I am unable to bear this people by myself; they are too heavy for me.

—Numbers 11:12-14

You can't just throw me out of here

Wait. Wait. What the hell are you doing, Dr Priestly? You can't just throw me out. You can't just inch me away from you as if I'm a little snail — 🐌 — or a tiny tapeworm in a retractable (intractable?) case

You want me to be a little separate? Well, I can't be separate if I've never been properly attached—can I? Am I too much for you? Oh no. No, no, no. You should keep holding me. You should hold me forever.

For ETERNITY

You are NOT allowed to miscarry me. My whole life was a miscarriage.

So now **U** have to make me feel held forever.

I am still a baby 🪨
No. Wait. I'm not a baby. I'm much more complex than that 🪨Ω

I feel so torn.
And it's you who are making me feel that way. So stop tearing us apart:
U tear us. UTERUS   **U** are tearing us apart

I cling to Dr Priestly because it's too dangerous to be pulled apart. Because why? Because: I don't want to be seen. I don't want to be face to face with her because then she'll see that I'm not so good, that I'm not good enough, not a fine and loving person. She'll see I'm bad. I can't bear it. It's too hard. I can't bear to take the measure of myself.

The Passover

Proximity to God is a dangerous affair:

And God said to Moses: And they shall take of the blood, and strike it on the door posts of the houses....And the blood shall be to you for a token upon the houses where you are; and when I see the blood, I will pass over you, and the plague shall not be upon you to destroy you, when I smite the land of Egypt—Exodus 12:7, 13

Π ▬

And this day shall be unto you for a memorial; and you shall keep it a feast to the Lord throughout your generations—Exodus 12:14

And the Exodus is a going out, a door way out. The blood on the door posts is a sign of this birth

(The house with the bloodless door way is the one to suffer the plague)

Is this just a pile of mush?

I have to say that being with Dr Priestly hasn't exactly been a picnic. Here I am, sitting in her reception room waiting for my session, endlessly waiting. She's late.

She really is impossible. I'm remembering back near the beginning of treatment when she all of a sudden raised her rates through the roof and I wanted to cut her head off. I'll never forget it. It got me so mad that I brought her one of my most awful dreams, the one about a decapitated head, down on the ground sticking out of the earth, like a *bloodless* mushroom, planted at the front door.

Π ✹

I raged and raged at her until I was blue in the face, I was screaming bloody murder—'off with your head!' because she'd raised my rate 140% can you believe it and here she was telling me her fee wasn't an emotional issue who is she kidding she's supposed to raise me up and instead she's giving herself a raise and then she says it shouldn't get a rise out of me on top of which she's demanding to know where's my body—meaning the body cut off in the dream—and then she caps off her whole enterprising wind-up by proclaiming: Yes Dr Priestly is 140% mushroom.

What a crazy volatile mushroom cloud of a lunatic she was. I think she and another patient had once gotten into such a hot-blooded blow-up that they ended up having to call the police. Can you imagine psychoanalysis becoming a matter for the police?

It was only much later that I realized maybe she'd been telling me she was 140% mush room.

Behold, this dreamer cometh

—Genesis 37:19

Birth

I forgot to mention that Dr Priestly has instructed me to draw the dream about my slinking around her bedroom. She often gives me Assignments to draw my dreams. She says the truth is in what I draw.

So, I sketch stick pins and write loving inscriptions in a kind of depth perspective and I add to the drawing whatever comes to mind: the entrance to a Tea House and a picture of a child eating an olive stuffed with a red pimento.

O-live it up, I think to myself.
Dr Priestly has one word to say about my dream drawing: **birth** ●

Well, how does she know? Is it because the red pimento looks like a red blooded umbilical cord? Something about the Tea House entrance—∏ a doorway through which one is born?

A few sessions later, she got up midway through the hour to get a cup of Tea. As she left the consulting room, a thin red belt fell off her waist onto the floor. She didn't stop to pick it up. Perhaps she didn't notice it?

I was astonished. It felt to me like the materialization of my dream drawing—of my red pimento and my Tea House. It felt like Dr Priestly was sleepwalking right through my dreams as though she was inside me.

Maybe it's that my dreams are inside her?

And the children of men take refuge in the shadow of thy wings,
For with thee is the fountain of life: in thy light do we see light

—Psalm 36   A Psalm of David

Behold. I make this as a covenant, Yahweh said, before all your people.
Watch yourself...lest you make covenants with those already in the land...Do
not bow down to another God, as if Jealous One is my name, Jealous Yahweh
—Exodus 34: 12-15

What psychoanalysis is all about

I think psychoanalysis is about giving birth to the child inside. Right? The analyst is a midwife. First, the patient's big head pops out between the analyst's legs and in that eternal instant, the analyst is a two-headed woman. She's the one, in that beginning, who has to do the thinking for the two of us   Or maybe the analyst is a catalyst who provides the nacre to help culture the baby pearl Maybe psychoanalysis is about making room in the world for the puny helpless child

Dr Priestly and I are making a baby together: a little gift to the world. A new me—a new beginning   But she's got to watch out how she does this because it's excruciating to admit how helpless I feel in the process—it's so weird, this relationship with a stranger really—a stranger to whom I belong. I mean I really do belong more and more to her in a sense. But meanwhile I can't seem to stop her from drawing out that puny part. I don't like that part—and I think it should stay hidden and unacknowledged.

But deep inside—under the bull of my raging veneer, I long to be borne in a good dream   Born from a warm womb   under a loving wing

It's as if she allows me to invent myself, create myself. I wish to be bold in the same way I envision her boldness, gliding on currents, from ice floe to ice floe on a cold green river—living at the edge, the electrifying edge. Maybe I can be like that river. She'd said I was like that river so springy and so green. Flow, flow, the current of life is ever onward. But if life and love are like a river, then they can't be hooked or pinned down like I'd been thinking. And then I can't control them. And that is a truly terrifying idea.

I hardly listen anymore to anybody but her. I rely on her. She's jealous about that, I think. And I'm glad because it means she cares deeply about me. So, when I'm scared, I remember her warm voice, her red telephone with its red blood cord of connection. She says I can call if I need to. And while I know in reality that I can't be her only special one—I mean she has her family and lots of patients, she has limits to her time— I still think she'll be there for me. She has enough love to go around. And with her love, I can allow myself to be born. Without her, I couldn't do it.

Yahweh spoke to Moses:

Carve two stone tablets and present yourself to me, on top of Mount Sinai... You will not bow down to another God, as if Jealous One is my name, Jealous Yahweh.... You write these words...

I am who brought you out of bondage

No false idols   No swear falsely   No murder...no steal...no covet

Honor Thy Father and Mother

—Exodus 20; 34: 1, 27

Trying to ⊘ buckle down

Dr Priestly says I'm trying to buckle down and be obedient. Her words make a boundary, a border around me, to help me feel safe. I need to feel safe because how else can I claim the past as my own? How else can I reconcile myself with it and have any faith in life? How else can I become unstuck and make a path for myself? Still, Dr Priestly's riding herd on me makes me nervous

Lots of things make me nervous. She says the violence of the past is still with me. My crazy lunatic parents—a father who didn't protect me, a crazy drunken mother. A mental case mother who nearly aborted me and called me a mistake

And when she got arrested and put in jail, when they booked her on a felony count for drunk driving and for bashing a policeman in the eye, I'm the one who had to go haul her out. Where was my father? How come he was never there when I needed him? Mother said he didn't love me. She said he couldn't find his way out of a paper bag.

That was mean. She was mean. But maybe she was right.

Somehow most everything between them was like a war, a war of either/or. And it was as if I was forced to choose between them, which meant that I was always betraying somebody.

And even though she was impossible, I chose my mother

The Golden Calf

Look. Now look:
Moses approaches the camp and sees the calf and the dancing.
His rage knows no bounds.
He hurls the tablets from his hands and smashes them at the foot
of the mountain.

—Exodus 32: 19

What counts in my book

When I was little, mother was always running around taking me with her to taverns, laughing with lots of strange men who were much more appealing to her than I was. And when they tried to put their bloody paws on her, I wanted to cut off their u-know-whats, I wanted to wring their necks   And hers too

Where was my father? Didn't he see those outright affairs, her flings right under his nose? Dr Priestly says he was a family man and that he had many worries. She said I was contemptuous. She said that it was *I* who didn't see *him*. Faithless, I must have been faithless

Dr Priestly is always weaving together good images of him with my feelings toward *her*. She brings him inside me with her. But I don't know. I don't think he loved me and I wanted to smash him and my past. And I'm terribly bitter about the time he smashed both mother and me to the ground, the time he belted us to the floor. In my book, *he* broke the law.

In my book, he was supposed to be wise and knowing, like a chief justice on the throne. But his own inner forces didn't allow him to see what was going on. And if he didn't want to see, then he didn't see. Maybe unconsciously *he's* the one who sent her to the taverns. He was so passive. People thought that he was nice and she was trouble but the way he held himself together was by laying low. He certainly was in no position to administer any law. He certainly wasn't in charge of any household. He was weak. And worse, he was retaliatory. You can't be a proper head of a household or a leader, if you're retaliatory. Sometimes he truly flipped out of control. In effect, my mother was the inmate running the asylum.

But growing up, I didn't take all this lying down. No. I carried on.
One summer, we'd had a mother's helper, Kitty, who talked back to my mother and put *her* in *her* place—from which I inferred: permission granted for me to become a little hell-raiser. Kitty and I grew so rambunctious that—while my baby brother ran naked through the woods—she high-tailed me all over the place piggyback and I yelled *gid'yip! gid'yip!*

Quite a mother's helper, Dr Priestly said.   Yes, well. What a zoo.

Balaam and the Talking Ass

Now Balaam saddled his Ass and went riding and the Ass saw the angel of the Lord standing in the way, with his sword drawn ⟶✦⟵ and the Ass laid down under Balaam and Balaam's anger was kindled and he smote the Ass

And the Lord opened the mouth of the Ass so that she said unto Balaam:
What have I done to you that you have smitten me?
And Balaam said: Because you have mocked me.

And the Ass said:
Am I not your own ass, on which you have ridden all your life?
Have I ever made an ass of you?

And he said: Nay

Then the Lord opened Balaam's eyes so that now he saw the angel standing in the way and he fell on his face and said: I have sinned; for I knew not that you stood in the way against me.

—Numbers 22:21-35

:

 Hold your horses interpreting my dreams

Dr Priestly has been running late for sessions again lately. It's extremely annoying and it's making me edgy. She's out parading around god knows where, making a mockery of my sitting waiting here in her place. Is this for real? Is she pulling my leg or what? It's making me crazy. Why should I have to wait on her? I'm not going to buckle under that smart ass old bag

I hate sitting here in her reception room, looking in the mirror. There's no way to avoid the mirror in here. I hate looking at myself. I don't want to see and I want her to just shut up. I could care less about understanding. All I want is her love, her unconditional love. And so what if my blindness results in my responding violently?   I mean just look around the world: half the world is in a blind rage so why should I have to be better, why should I be different?

Besides, meanwhile I've dreamt a good dream, no thanks to her:

I'm a frisky little horse running around with
the incredibly interpretive power of dreams.
I'm wearing a dream pail around my neck. The pail
looks likes a horse feedbag—or maybe a garbage bag

Well, I am like a little horse running around, frisky and full of life. And I'm ever so fed up being saddled with her interpretations, her readings of my Tea leaves. She thinks I don't bridle at her instruction and Assignments? I'll sack every inch of her training: **Look Ma, no hands!** So get off your high horse Dr Priestly—I'm more neck-and-neck, more eye-2-eye with you than you think. I'm not your little hobbyhorse.

And I'm not going to be stuck on you, stuck with you, smitten by you
You old tea bag, old heehaw nag

My Lord He calls me. He calls me by the thunder—American Spiritual

STEEL AWAY

I'm full of life, am I not? Am I not full of it?

I'm not exactly sure I'm being honest. So Dr Priestly tells me honesty is the wrong word for someone who goes around blindly.

She speaks of my self-hatred—my trashing myself. She says I'm overwhelmed and that I don't consider reality, I attempt to defeat it.

I steel myself against the world. I continue to brace myself against reality. It's too painful. I don't want to be touched by the painful things that can come out. It's better to embroider little stories, even if maybe they're a stack of lies

Ever since I was little, I made a mountain of such stories. When I was really little I concocted the idea that you could shit a baby. I thought that's how babies popped out. They were like candy Brown Babies. You could get them by the box-load like treats from a slot machine, like pennies from piggybanks. I could have lots and lots of them

Later, it struck me that making a baby really hurts—and I mean much more than a pin prick

to draw blood ● A body could be torn to pieces. Making a baby could be like sticking a giant safety pin in a girl's belly button. Making a baby could be like a thunderbolt or streak of lightning that descends into the muck to light up an egg like a pearl

But on the other hand it could happen that the whole ruddy mess could get sizzled and fried.

And that's how I felt growing up when father berated my painful periods calling me weak like his mother for which I hated him with a hatred that doubled me over in pain despite Midol. It sent me headlong spinning on the pavement, it tarred me in the miscarriage of oh my God it's a girl. I'm a girl.

Stolen Idols

When Jacob finally readied to return to the land of Canaan,

his beloved wife Rachel carried off her father's idols
and stashes them in the saddle cushions.

And now she sits on the stolen idols

Her father comes to search for them, but finds nothing.

She says to him:

Let my lord not take it amiss if I do not appear beside you.
But I am in the way of women——my period ● is with me

—Genesis 31:34-35

Miscarried?

Dr Priestly is a girl. A woman, a mature woman—Does it have to mean a barren wasteland with nothing there? There's no wee wee there, just a hole? She tells me to think of it as a white light

I never met anyone as strong as Dr Priestly is. So feminine, so receptive—yet, she's a better man than most (including my father).

She says I needn't feel envious. She says I have my own radiance. She says I'm a diamond when I'm relaxed and that anybody can see that. Well, I say, a gem, okay, but what about a penis? I don't have a penis. She says I'm an artist.

I like her brand of mettle. I can see I've warmed up to her good-natured sturdiness. I see I have an impact on her.

But if I'm so artistic, so gifted and full of light, how come I feel so impoverished? How come the story of my life—the under-story of my life—feels like a garbage heap, a miscarriage, a bloody mess? I've had another odd dream—I think I like it but I'm not sure. In this one, I'm full of babies. But, side-by-side with that, I'm having my period:

I dream I'm planted firmly on the Earth—barefoot
and naked. My insides are filled with baby birds.
Little foxes curl up inside my elbows. Newts
and salamanders frolic inside my arms. A diamond
of blood is covering my private parts

What kind of fix is this? Maybe it's not the blood of a miscarriage? Maybe it's about coming of age? Maybe the dream is innocent of time—the dream exists in eternal time—so that no sooner than I come of age and begin menstruating, I get pregnant? pregnant and filled with life? I don't know. That doesn't seem very promising. Maybe I'm just very confused.

Be fruitful and multiply

"(In Genesis) the desire for blessing represented a longing for the superabundant life—chiefly manifest in fertility: human beings and animals alike were to be fruitful, were to multiply—Their progeny would bring them immortality—The divinely given fecundity would enable men and women to triumph over death....Blessing was neither effortlessly bestowed nor effortlessly received (but often enough)...was dominated by anxiety about the Promise, which seemed constantly in danger of miscarrying"   —*In the Beginning*

God blessed them, saying,
Be fruitful, and multiply, and fill the waters in the seas,
and let the birds fly above the earth—Genesis 1:22

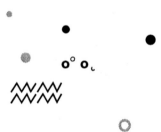

Egad, What a Commanding Bris!!

Go again to Egypt, God said to Moses.

On the way, at a night lodging place,
God met Moses——and was ready to kill him●

Then Zipporah took a flint and cut off her son's foreskin——
and touched it between Moses' legs●

Surely you are my blood bridegroom, she said,
a blood bridegroom marked by this circumcision

—Exodus 4:24-26

— ● —

Under ◆ Story

There's another half to my dream of babies. But I'm embarrassed to tell it because it seems so cold, so cut-off and castrating. Maybe it really nails how bad I am. But what did I do that was *so* bad? What is so bad?

I dream I'm planted firmly on the Earth—naked.
My body's filled with babies....A diamond of blood◆
is covering my private parts. And next to me, Man
is standing naked. He reveals a drop of blood ●
at the tip of his penis. The blood is expressed
as breast milk—in identification with me.

It wasn't until years later that the richness of this dream struck me. And only then did the thought occur that the blood on the tip is a circumcision, a bris.

And then I thought how a woman's biology is so much about **blood.** And painful as that is, blood is connected with the gift of birth, with babies and creativity.

At the same time, blood is what is shed on the cross; "it" is what people drink at communions, shockingly archaic though that seems. Blood is connected with sacrifice and bonding. Like when we were little and we became blood brothers.

And so I think the circumcision in my dream—and in life—is like that. Its ritual is a kind of becoming human. It's a way that *he* mirrors the biological suffering *she* endures. Perhaps that's how it is between psychoanalyst and patient.

And I think the two dream figures—male and female side by side are like two stone tablets carved in stark relief— each silently self-contained, so innocent— like Adam and Eve—mirroring each other, imbued with each other. Different from each other yet sufficiently alike as to be comprehensible, each to the other

The Holy One desires the heart—The Talmud

A Play for the Heart

But it's true I'm so cold. I got arrested, stopped, frozen dead in my tracks because when I was little, on top of other unfortunate things that happened to me, my heart got cut out of my body. It happened when I went for a Tonsillectomy.

They had to cut my throat and to me it meant they cut my voice out of my throat. And so, my heart got cut out in little pieces because it was attached by golden threads to my voice. I thought a metronome with a tootsie pop top went in the place where my heart had been. I thought the tootsie gyrated wildly in a sea of blood in my mouth. And it was around that time that I began to wonder about the cruel taller beings who lorded over me. I wondered: Do adults possess a heart?

And to this day I've feared I have no heart. Only a metronome

Dr Priestly has me imagine my imaginary heart talking to another heart, a

mirrored heart:

Heart says to mirrored heart:
Can I touch you?   Yes. You can. You will.

When Dr Priestly is with me, things are bound to look different because of her heartfelt mirroring. I imagine looking into her eyes, seeing myself in her eyes, seeing through her world full of light and wondering if she sees herself in my eyes: eye-in-infinite-eye. I imagine my metronome dreaming of being transformed into a firefly wand as though *it* could become Earth's metronome—as though *its* dream could pry open the eternal night sky—full of fireflies and stars— to summon the music of the spheres.   But when I'm alone, I can hardly imagine any such thing

Still, I think right then it was beginning to dawn on me that psychoanalysis is a play for the heart. It's a drama—it's a play for the heart and its dreams.

The Binding of Isaac

And God said to Abraham: Take now thy son, thine only son Isaac, whom thou lovest, and get thee to Mount Moriah ▲

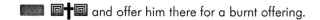 and offer him there for a burnt offering.

So Abraham took Isaac and the wood and the fire in his hand and a knife. And Isaac said to him: Behold the fire and wood — but where is the lamb for a burnt offering?

Abraham bound Isaac, his son, and laid him on the altar
Abraham stretched forth his hand—took the knife to slay his son

—Genesis 22: 2, 6-10

Cutlass?

A lot of stuff—like the Tonsillectomy—hadn't meant much to me before my treatment with Dr Priestly. I'd blanked a lot out. But in her presence, we entered the playhouse of my deepest fears and somehow things were brought mentally into relief—as if excised in stone or *italicized to tell it slant* or maybe boldly **red lettered**, like some odd piece of Good News:

I was 8 and it was the first winter snowstorm at our new house. Mother and I heard strange noises upstairs. It sounded like closet doors sliding open—except there weren't any sliding doors upstairs. Mother took a knife and she took me. We mounted the stairs to look in the attic closet for the Thing that was Making us Nervous. Mother kept me at her side as she swung open the attic door

I stood stock still as she wielded the knife in an arc over my head
No. Nobody. Nothing there—Mistake. Noise—what? The noise was just icicle shards sliding down the roof's slope.

But what was in mother's head? Why—why did she go up there at all? Why didn't she call the police? And why did she take me with her? Was *I* supposed to protect *her*? Dr Priestly mused: *perhaps I'd felt that the knife was meant for me.*

And that made me think somehow mother had the idea to cut me off—(off with my head!)—cut me, cut her daughter out of the picture like she'd cut herself out of the picture—because really, as an orphan placed in foster care, she *had* truly been cut out of the picture. And without help, she couldn't help repeating what had been done to her. And I—in my cutting and cut-off ways, I—in turn, was repeating what had been done to me. And I was going to have to stop. I'd have to face up, to wake up, to the music.

I'd have to wake up and start thinking about the things that make me nervous. It's true I'd been cut out of the picture when I was little. But now, Dr Priestly was helping me make a new picture. And I didn't have to cut myself out of the picture. I didn't have to be stuck in that bind any more. Right? I mean, it might take me forty years but I was going to fix this picture. I was going to repair the cut, the tear in the veil of my being.

Thicket

"The Aqedah incident (the word 'aqedah' means 'binding'), in which Abraham almost sacrifices Isaac to Yahweh, (is) the ultimate model for the slaughter of Jesus as the Lamb of God"   **—Jesus and Yahweh The Names Divine**

"According to Carl Jung, Melito of Sardis (2nd century) taught that Christ the Lamb was comparable to the ram caught in the thicket that Abraham sacrificed in place of his son, and that the thicket represented the Cross."
                    —Symbols of Transformation

"Isaac's life (was) a blank after his father bound him on the altar and came at him with a knife. It is...not surprising that he called God 'the Fear' (Genesis 31:42, 53)....The passive Isaac is acted upon, duped (by his son Jacob) and constantly presented to us as on the brink of death....In the two most important scenes of Isaac's life he is lying down—on the altar of sacrifice, and on his deathbed."   **—In the Beginning**

Mistakes

It's so hard coming here and lying down on this couch, wrestling with this stuff. I mean sometimes I feel I'm coming unglued, unraveled. It's so painful hearing her tell me how passive I am, how pathetically locked up inside myself. I feel like she can see right through me. I feel like when I was little and they put me in that x-ray machine and all I could hear was its horrid eery buzz and all I could see was its screen that seemed to peel away my flesh and blood and prove the death of me.

But I'm beginning to see, even if I'm often tied in knots and even if half of what I say is bullshit, that I can make a lot more connections. I'm seeing that maybe what has felt true might not actually be real. I'm noticing that I've made a lot of mistakes in how I've pieced together my picture of the world. I'm noticing that my stubborn insistence is more often a result of my nervousness about my own uncertainty than of anything else. I've constantly insisted that I see the heart of the matter, whatever the matter is. And now I'm noticing that I might not have a clue about the heart of certain matters. That's not an easy thing to admit. Even though in a way, it's a relief.

And I guess it makes sense. I mean I was a child when, in my own odd and frightened way, I put together the puzzling pieces of the world around me, without anybody much helping me to make sense out of what was going on. I lived in a fuzzy little fantasy world. Maybe I'm still living in a fantasy world and I don't even know it. Anyway, it's good that I can come in here and talk to Dr Priestly and acknowledge my regrets (I mean, who honestly doesn't have regrets in life?) and I can tell her all kinds of thorny stuff nobody else ever seemed much interested in hearing. I can come here, here to confront myself, confront the dark night of the soul, and the lightness too.

That red-letter day

I've been telling Dr Priestly more about when I was 8 years old and the day we moved to our new house. Just the other night, I had a dream about wanting help from The Fishing Supply Company—and it reminded me of that moving day.

It was nearly 100 degrees that June summer day we moved to a small fishing town on an island. We stopped first at the local heating oil Company so that father could arrange a Supply hook-up and I remember sitting in the back seat of our Plymouth panting like a little cat with my sandpaper tongue hanging out in the heat, I was dripping, melting like a little butter stick, my ears buzzing with the high pitched mid-day sound of cicadas or maybe they were bees.

It was a relief to arrive at our house, so cool inside—we opened all the windows and the door ∏ that gave out onto a miracle of green. We had a picnic on the living room floor. Mother had made delicious devilled eggs which father and I gobbled up—all yellow and soft and sprinkled with Hungarian red paprika. ● ₒ Mother's adoptive father who died when she was young had been Hungarian and a good cook so that's why, even though her birth parents she'd never met had been Russian, she was always using so much red paprika

We had a mortgage and a new deed instead of the older one that had said: No Jews Allowed.

After the picnic, I met the next-door children who'd moved there on that very same **red-letter day**. They told me they were Roman Catholic and that their mother said I was a Jew and that Jews had murdered their Lord Jesus Christ. I had no idea what they were talking about. I was speechless.

That was a long summer. I felt empty and lonely and I needed Company. Mother was lonely too and depressed. (Dr Priestly told me, years later, that mother most likely suffered from manic depression) And father was away a lot on business. The best thing that happened was I got a bicycle that I could ride all over the island, fast as the wind, and I named him Fury.

I am the voyce of a cryar in the wilderness
—Sancte Jhon 1:23

"He told me once that being blessed meant being bloodied, and that
is true etymologically speaking, in English—but not in Greek or Hebrew.
So whatever understanding might be based on that derivation has no
scriptural authority behind it" — Gilead

Take the pain away ✚

I think maybe I'm ready to check into a Hospital. Really, I can't take this anymore. I can't bear all this exposure—these feelings of weakness and vulnerability. I think I have to wrap this pain in gauze binding ▓. I have to burrow up to my neck in gauze linen. I have to make the pain go away, disappear.

I feel so split apart, so torn. One part functions well. But the other hidden part, a foreign part, a fringe—the puny cut off child that turns out somehow to be the creative part, the heart of me— still remains somehow inaccessible—as if crying out from a tomb. I think it's time to get out of here.

When my baby brother was being born, the slithery blood cord got wrapped around his neck and nearly killed him. At his birth, they gave me a baby doll and I thought to smear honey on its belly button ● I could smear honey like a salve on the severed place—where it ached.

Now I'm thinking of my dollhouse, toy-theater of my childhood in which I cast myself as God of midolls ⚲ I was their idol, their cause for thanksgiving. I pleased my little supplicants by bringing gifts—like the gifts I bring Dr Priestly. I brought miniature toy roasted meats and red wine bottles and tiny silver platters with toy wine glasses and tiny books to read.

I knew all about the wars in the world so I sent the boy dolls out to fight. When they got wounded, I wrapped gauze linen ▓ on their injuries and daubed them with Mercurochrome ● to fix them up. This was my idea of Doll Hospital✚. This was the bloodied aspect of my consciousness. This was my belief that what was good would be cut off.

For the maide is not dead, but slepeth—Mathew 9:24

Playing Possum

I'm thinking back to when I was even littler and I kept my nose in my book, pretending not to hear what was going on around me. I'm remembering how I especially loved the drawings of a baby possum who was suspended in my favorite childhood book—his scribbly little body touched my heart, hanging there in a tree eternally upside-down all alone.

I seem to somehow recall overhearing mother bitterly complaining to her friend that father wasn't good…but money, children…and how Henriette (mother's adoptive mother) had wrongly hidden mother's birthright and how now the truth came out that she'd been adopted and now Henriette was at Hospital because she went crazy when mother discovered the lies about the past. *And twenty-six shock treatments later the fat horse still keeps ranting.* Nothing shuts her up. So mother must cut her off because she is so bad.

While mother went on, I pretended to read how humans think the little possum is frowning. But I knew they were making a big mistake since he hung upside down in his tree. He was all the while a smiling baby.

I wish I could be with Dr Priestly right now, curled up on her couch. I wish I didn't feel so lost, so pained. She would relieve me. She would go with me in these places, be there waiting for me when I got there, crouching down with me when I felt all alone when I got there she'd make it into a secure hold.

Π†

CLOV: Do you believe in the life to come?
HAMM: Mine was always that.
                              —Endgame

Still born

I'm sitting here in her reception room waiting for my session to begin, what else is new. Looking in the mirror ⭕ there's no place to sit in this space so that the mirror is avoidable. I still hate looking in the mirror, looking at myself. Looking at my eyes: eye-2-eye, an eye-4-an-eye, 4-eyes. Right from the beginning with her, she was following me with her mirror. She wanted me to be able to see myself. Now look—look at this, look at that.

It's evening now and the light is dim. And she's running late. And it's getting darker, a lot darker.   Stuck, I feel stuck. Hurry up already. It's time What's she doing? What on earth is she doing?

Now I've become aware that I'm singing a song to myself: *Honey pie, you are driving me crazy.* Actually, my heading is pounding. She told me my headaches are the bully, the tormentor, in me: I *should*. I *must*. She said when I started feeling pity, fear and compassion, my head would stop hurting.

Sometimes in session instead of lying there helplessly on my back facing up, I

like to flip over. I mean how can a person take all this lying down? < 🔹▬ >

I think maybe it's safer to flip onto-all-4s < 🔹Ω > with my back up. I'm probably the only patient in history who flips this way, but this way I can keep an eye on her 👤[🔹Ω]

How else could I avoid being laid low by all these strange memories, strange dreams and this even stranger psychoanalyst? It's a little like trying to leave the pangs of childbirth on the labor room table by flipping onto-all-4s and bursting out the words: I'm getting the hell out of here.

There are a surprising number of doorways in and out of this reception room. How many rooms are there in this place, anyway? Only kidding. But in truth, I don't move. I'm sitting here immobilized—as if stuck—as if stapled or sutured— to the chair, as if I might be swept up in a whirlwind the moment I go through the double doors into her consulting room.

Π   ΠΠ Π   ΠΠΠ   ΠΠΠ   Π   Π

The people grumbled [about Moses] saying: What shall we drink?

Why did you lift us out of Egypt? Was it to die of thirst?

Our spirit dries looking at nothing but manna.

Why did we ever come out from Egypt?

Is God with us—or not?

Moses said to Yahweh: Perhaps you will forgive their contempt; if not, erase me—bless heaven—from the book you have written. Yahweh answered: Whoever has contempt for me, I will blot out from my book. I'll give you the tablets I've written for instruction. Make me an offering, a Tabernacle—a portable Sanctuary in the wilderness

—Exodus 15: 24; 17:3, 7; 32: 32-33

Peek

I'm so sick I could die. This is too hard. My head is splitting, my temples throbbing. Lately, Dr Priestly has been canceling sessions back-to-back. I have no idea what she thinks of me. Am I erased from her book? from her calendar?

I learn she has a thyroid problem. Thy roid and thy staff, they do not comfort me.

I feel so abandoned. And I've dreamt of taking a sneak peek at Dr Priestly's write-ups from our sessions. In the dream, I can hardly make out her inscrutable handwriting. It seems as obscure as my father's affection for me.

She asks me to draw the dream. So, I create a locket out of a Tea Ball— like a portable charm or a girl's toy pocket-book, a wire mesh toy (tea) bag. I nestle two round miniatures I've painted into the locket so that they peek out through the wire mesh scrim, as if in a kind of screened play. One painting is a self-portrait and the other is handwritten psychoanalytic text.

And somehow I think the Tea Ball has to do with unveiling myself through the wire mesh screen and maybe brewing something—side-by-side with Dr Priestly. Something illuminating that I can carry with me, carry with me always—something to do with becoming more human, something to do with the birth of law and love

With honey from the rock, I will satisfy you — Deuteronomy 32:13
(The Song of Moses)

The time she called me honey

It was hard sometimes not to feel like I was drowning in treatment. It was hard not to feel the stings of Dr Priestly's observations, her forceful interpretations.

But then there were the times she said things that softened my heart, things no one else had ever said to me. Like the time she called me honey and told me how wonderful I am.

After that, I went home and threw up all over the place because I couldn't digest the love.

Or the time we talked about being alone. I told her that to me, being alone meant Exile. Abandonment—Alone was a barren desert

But she said to her it meant sitting by herself in summer, on an island, in the heather on the hill—with bees buzzing around.

 And then I wished I could be there too. That was when she said: To be alone is a gift—the precious gift of individuality

Terrified of Being

I've been dreaming a lot of bees. Be not afraid   I'm Terrified.
I'm scared to death of being

I'm sure Dr Priestly put these dreams in me—as if by a sting operation—Buzzing in my ear about bees in the heather on the hill   Piercing my ear, making my ear ring   It's too hard to change, to become human, to uncover myself. So hard to open up. I'm tormented. I feel something bad is coming but I don't know what.

And as for her, she's the bane of my existence. Both bane and balm
••

Bees are everywhere in the dream—circling around me.
They're all over me. I'm totally astonished •

Then I dream that a honey bee buzzing round my head
lands inside my ear —-creeps into my middle ear—
If I move it will sting. I try to sound the word HELP
without stirring up any reverberation.

Paralyzed, I whisper: 'how to get the bee out? ' ◀

Am I the ear? Am I the bee? Yes. Are these my own angry words—or Dr Priestly's—fighting words? words buzzing in on me. She's getting under my skin, under my bee veil, with all her stinging observations. She's driving me crazy. She better cut it out. •

Next dream: I'm cleaning a cup that's shaped liked an ear. Inadvertently, I
disrupt the bee bane—the hibernating bee • balm—that's curled up inside. The
curlicues are like layers of encrusted wings all yellow gold, and black. Suddenly
little bees • *start coming out at me. They sting my arms, my legs—I could have*
a heart attack. The bee venom could kill me

And it came to pass at the time of the offerings of the evening sacrifices…

—1 Kings 18:36

Let me go
I will not let go, unless you bless me

—Genesis 32: 26

Invitation to an evening bash

I think these evening sessions— or should I call them

evening bashes?—mad Tea Balls—these twilight 'festfights'
o° o₍

of ours— are driving me CRAZY

I can't bear them. They're killing me. All this exposure is killing me. She's

killing me. What does she want? What?   She wants me to

enter into the dance of life?

I don't know if I can do it.

I don't know if I can follow her lead.

She's too inscrutable, too foreign   Insufferable.

She might even be downright un-American

Let me out of here

Whither thou goest I will go, whither thou stayest I will stay
For your people will be my people and your God my God....

—The Book of Ruth 1: 16

Now what? What's she up to now? Now I see what it is: Here I am struggling like hell to give birth to love and law inside myself. Here I am doing everything I can to come to life and make myself lovable. Here I am going crazy (she's driving me crazy) and now she says that **she** needs to go away to rest. She's going away to an island (right, sure…to sit on a hill with bees buzzing around). It's not right of her.

She shouldn't go. I don't want her to go off like that, so separate from me. It's making me seasick. I want her to be *with* me. She's supposed to come to my rescue and take care of me. Or take me with her

She says I can write her letters and send them to her home address

Why would I send things to her home address? She won't even be home. I want to be able to reach her. So I quoted to her what Ruth said in the bible to her Mother-in-Law, the part about how Ruth sacrifices herself to follow her Mother-in-Law, how Ruth sacrifices the precious gift of her individuality:

Whither thou goest I will go, whither thou stayest I will stay
 For your people will be my people and your God my God…

So Dr Priestly joked that it might be best not to tell me *which* hilly island she was going to because she was afraid I might follow her there…Very funny

Sigmund Freud, referring to the hypothesis of another author, had a further surmise in **Moses and Monotheism:**

"(The author) found in the book of the Prophet Hosea unmistakable traces of a tradition to the effect that the founder of their religion, Moses, met a violent end in a rebellion of his stubborn and refractory people. The religion he had instituted was at the same time abandoned.

Let us adopt...the surmise that the Egyptian Moses was killed by the Jews, and the religion he instituted abandoned. It allows us to spin our thread further...."

YOU're leaving ME? Are you crazy?

But really I'm so pissed off that she has vacated the premises on holiday and left me alone.

Maybe I should just quit. I should sever the relationship.
It's much too all-consuming anyway.

And think of all the money I'll save. And all the work I won't have to do

I could say to her: YOU'RE FIRED. You can't just leave me in the lurch.

YOU'RE FIRED. And no severance for you

Part 2

Embracing the Self

(I'm really not crazy)

For my mother [gave me falsehood], but my true [mother] gave me life
—Gospel of Thomas 101

"What really is birth? This relates to the enigmatic saying 101 (of
Thomas), where the 'true' mother evidently is distinguished from
 the natural or actual mother" —*Where Shall Wisdom be Found?*

My mother

I've been spending a lot of time this summer thinking about my mother. I've been thinking about the things she loves: nature and Leonard Bernstein and dancing and beautiful clothes and hot dogs and gardenias and so many wonderful pleasures in life and how she used to run around acting like a celebrity, wishing to be a celebrity like Elizabeth Taylor playing Cleopatra and how sometimes when she'd had too much to drink she'd start talking in a slurry southern accent and then a British accent, how when I was growing up, she'd call me pussycat one minute and pull my clothes out of the closet and throw them all over the floor the next.

When I was young, we used to go walking in the cool of the evening and then she would tell me what was beautiful in the world and I clung to her then and she would point to the glow of light and peace that emanated from other people's houses. And I knew what an unusual eye, an original eye, she had and how strange she was and I knew it was excruciating—how lost she felt.

I'm thinking how she'd disappeared for days on some binge or other and how, years later, I took her to an institution and she wanted to check right in and it made me cry. She wanted help and she knew she needed it. Later she thanked me for having taken her there, for having helped her do something for herself

But a few months of help weren't enough. She needed so much more, so very much more. And really, she wanted me to take care of her. And what a hard time I'd had because sometimes I just wanted to punch her. I just wanted her to stop. I couldn't take it. I've been at such a loss sometimes about how to be with her. I love her and yet being with her has made me cringe. But Dr Priestly has been teaching me how to be a better person, a better daughter

So many things in my life have turned out to be so difficult, so uncertain. When I was a younger woman, I'd thought I'd escaped my childhood unscathed. But that turned out to be totally untrue. How I made it as well as I did—how so many of us make it—is, in some sense, a wonder. I wish so much it had been different.

Dr Priestly told me I was strong. And she has spoken to me of the wisdom of uncertainty. So maybe this summer, while she's away, I can sometimes sit under a tree and ponder the wisdom of uncertainty.

A new beginning

He happened on a place where a flock of birds filled the air. And there, under a tree, the monk known as Saint Francis of Assisi communed with his little brother birds and blessed them. Susceptible to his charms, the birds entered into loving companionship with him. Even the half-frozen bees crawled toward him in the winter, seeking to be fed.

He delighted in corresponding with earth's creatures, in singing canticles of praise to brother Sun and sister Moon. Although Francis had wasted his youth, he was able to make a new beginning—able to renounce the material world around him, for a simpler life of devotion and good works

He passed the hours of this life on earth by following in the steps of Christ, by devoting himself to helping the needy and healing the sick.

This correspondence of ours ◎ ⋀⋀ ⌂

Dr Priestly is back from her island holiday and I've had such an entrancing dream (I think it's about her but maybe it means *I'm* entrancing too?)—except it's giving me a terrible ear ache

The dream is set on "Monk Island"—as in something monkish? It's somehow medieval and monastic; as an ivy covered tower in nature; as a beehive city in nature, and ascetic (like Francis of Assisi?). It's priestly! It's Dr Priestly! Yes and it even includes a tiny symphony of bells, reminiscent of an Ingmar Bergman film of a charming seaside clock shop:

I'm on an island—Monk Island. I turn on many
kinds of music clocks, music boxes, antique bells in
towers, wind chimes, wind-up carousel clocks, a Tree
of Life clock last played when Peter Minuet came
to visit. The noise—incredibly loud—ears chiming

I wake up with the slightly alarming feeling that my heart is clanging in my throat. It feels like while I slumber, the dream blossoms. The dream is a flower that comes to life at night. It dances off the wall and tries to pin its bouquet of notes on me, as it calls out:

🕺 Hey wallflower, shall we dance? Let's dance!

I know what this dream is: it's a big celebration of Dr Priestly's return. She's finally back so now we can start again! It's a dance, a minuet, to a little night music. My head is its music box—like the music box I once gave Dr Priestly as a gift (it played *eine kleine nacht musick*). Also, the dream resembles an antique charm—it slips its music into me to ward off my destructiveness, to ward off my anger at her having gone away on her island vacation.

But now I'm more receptive to some sort of altering experience. Maybe up above my head, I hear music in the air. My ear chamber and the psychoanalytic chamber are corresponding better. And the dream rings out the evidence of my increasing devotion to this kind of resonance.

his Book of Hours

Portable and personal, Books of Hours were used during the Middle Ages for daily prayer and recitation of psalms and hymns. They were a testament to the importance of religious devotion in daily life. And they reflected the wish of ordinary people to incorporate the monastic practices of monks and nuns into everyday experience.

In the same way that church bells summoned the faithful to prayer, Books of Hours conducted people through the daily cycle of canonical hours, helping them secure salvation, helping them answer their need for a clear and ordered path through life.

Produced by hand, Books of Hours were often given as gifts. Frequently, they included miniature paintings and textual ornamentation known as illumination

.

My head is a cuckoo clock

Actually, I have NO idea what I'm doing dreaming about monks.
But my Monk Island dream is so resonant I can nearly touch its humming
vibrations. Maybe dreams are like bees humming in a hive—or like birds—little
birds from foreign worlds. Little pearls from foreign worlds.

Dr Priestly says: Every dream is a world. That's a beautiful idea—like when she
speaks of learning to swim in the deep without drowning .Or when she says that
perhaps we will write a book together someday

I wish I had a capacity like hers to embrace the world, to be devoted the way she
is. Maybe I could be like a nun flying around in the bells of St Mary's or like
Sister Wendy on an art tour. Or like Francis of Assisi who'd seemed so charming
but now strikes me as quite an odd bird.

I think this Monk dream is really quite a little duet, somewhere between *Tea for
Two* and *Let's Do It*. Two strangely humming birds—*Birds do it, bees do it*—two
bees going toe-to-toe on the entry plank to the hive—Dr Priestly and I are those
bee bopping strange birds on the landing board of my tongue—calling out the
hours from my cuckoo clock head. Dr Priestly is dancing around at the door way
singing: This way to the honey! This way to the flowers, honey!

You're impossible but I love you anyway

Dr Priestly hasn't been shy about letting me know how far I've fallen short as a daughter. I mean, in the sense that it's time for me to take care of my mother. She has taught me in so many ways how to be with my mother —how to get to know my mother, how to be my own inner mother. Dr Priestly has given me plenty of lessons in goodness, plenty of assistance in the art of living. Hopefully, I'm more able to incorporate this goodness into myself, forever, so I'll know what to do with myself and my mother. I won't be at a loss anymore.

Sometimes, instead of getting so exasperated that I want to wring mother's neck, I repeat to her the words Dr Priestly taught me: You're impossible but I love you anyway. And it works like a charm. Mother stops dead in her tracks and starts laughing out loud. How great is that

When she suggested telling it to mother, it hadn't occurred to me that maybe that's how Dr Priestly thinks about *me*. I only thought of that later. Truthfully, many things I say to mother fail miserably and I've begun to see it's because the things I say and how I say them have been neither honest nor empathic. Apparently, I haven't mastered even the most basic rudiments in the art of living.

I confess to being so self-absorbed as to not pay attention to my mother's plight. I've been cold and callous and were it not for Dr Priestly, I'd most likely have gone right on being that way. But I do feel sad for my poor mother. Very sad and I want to help her. And we've put in an application for her at Land's End, which is a wonderful continuum care place. I mean as wonderful as any such place could be. When I'd originally broached the subject and we visited it, mother said: *Sign me up for the royal suite!* But there's a long waiting list and in any event, I don't know if they'd accept her. And even *if* we get her in there— which I have every intention of doing, would they keep her? In five minutes, she could start acting up and they could want to throw her out. Can a person be evicted from Assisted Living? from Assistance in Living?

It's hard to think that after all my struggles in life, all my attempts to improve myself, that I'm ending up spending all my free time putting rubber sheets on mother's bed or plowing through mountains of her accumulated paperwork and writing out checks to pay her bills or bringing her M&Ms and other junk she likes. But I love my mother. And really, she is basically good at heart.

In my father's house are many mansions — John 14:2

Blessings to all who enter here

Now cast your nets wherever you wish—never afeard are we…
And some folks thought it was a dream they'd dreamed ◀
Of sailing that beautiful sea—Dutch Lullaby

Safety Net

Sometimes I'm so exasperated with my lack of empathy. Why can't I take Dr Priestly's compassion into myself? I've spent so much time carrying on about how *she's* not taking *me* in. But really it's the reverse: the truth is *I'm* not taking *her* in. Well, now I've dreamt that *she's an artistic correspondent noting the sorry state of my shoes and wounded feet*. The dream setting is a *fish restaurant*—like the shoes of the fisherman?

In session she notes how competitive and ambitious I am. And then I tell her all I ever do is carry on and that when I was little I longed for my mother to stay and read me bedtime stories and lullabies like **Wyncken, Blyncken and Nod**, the Fishermen Three, and all the fish that live in the beautiful sea but how she went off and left me and I was afraid of the dark and Dr Priestly said I never carried on about her leaving me. Actually, that's true. I never even thought of doing so.

Here now—within the 4 walls of the psychoanalytic chamber—all I need to do is let go and follow her lead. But it's not something I can *will*. It only happens when I'm ready. So frustrating—but at least even if I resist what she puts in my path, things have a way of seeping in, germinating—taking root under the cover of evening sessions

I can see how a psychoanalytic chamber resembles a house with many rooms— many mansions. Whether an ear chamber or temple of the mind; a redressing room; a birthing room, (a uterus). Or, on bad days, it's a chamber pot—a pail for refuse. When I cry it's a blue room—when I'm exploding, it's a mushroom; and certainly it's more breathing room than I ever had before. But: can I find room for love inside the chamber of my heart? Can I be more patient? More of a patient—one cannot be an impatient patient.

Let me just lay down my arms and put whatever remains of my temple-throbbing rage in her hands. I'm secure here in her chamber. Lying here on this couch, this little ship of state, facing the double doors of her consulting room, facing the wall surrounding the double doors, the wall filled with assorted paintings of Madonna and child, the crucifixion, a fisherman with a fishing net— Lying here on this couch, I'm next to the safety net of her, a precious connection

A fisher of men

Come follow me, and I will make you fishers of men.
And at once, they left the nets and followed him.

—Matthew 4: 19-20

Duccio: The Calling of the Apostles

Yesterday
I learned Dr Priestly's husband died suddenly. I was shocked. I felt so helpless. Then, at the funeral service, there was a memorial card that read:

> Come follow me, and I will make you fishers of men.
> And at once, they left the nets and followed him.

It made me think of my fish restaurant dream. And about the Fishermen Three, Wyncken, Blyncken and Nod—and I felt that our dreams and longings are connected, hers and mine—and really, all of us, we're all of us like waves in the sea, we're like the fish that live in the beautiful sea

During the service, Dr Priestly's face was covered with a small veil. And that reminded me of the time she visited me in Hospital and she wore a dress that revealed her wonderful warm bosom except it was covered with a veil and I was reminded how in the bosom of my family there was no bosom and then I thought about my father's terribly small funeral so long ago. And too, all of this—I mean the death and funeral, made me think of mother's increasing fragility and how ridiculously transitory everything is.

I had no words—only a terrible sense of Dr Priestly's loss—later I wrote a poem to give her. It was about bees. Earth's beehive hymn

I was consoled when I wrote it. I felt connected to the physical aliveness of the earth, the shimmering sensation of bees humming in their hive, their city in nature. I felt as though I could see all the molecules of the air weaving in and out the trees, the grass, the leafy world of nature that I love. I could make choices about the words that inspire me, many choices. My poem ended with the thought: No such thing as immortality. Yet, deep from the hive's round right well—embodied voices spring

And I thought it was good, this idea of embodiment. I felt I do have a voice. It hadn't been cut out of my throat. Or if it had, it was being restored. And I thought there was some authority in my voice

By what authority doest thou these things
and who gave thee this power?

—Matthew 21:23

Torch Song

I dreamt that father has come back from the dead. A fire torch burns at the doorway. Ghosts climb the stairs. Father is in the rafters—he drops a dollhouse-sized silver platter for cupcakes into my lap. I cry out loud: 'father, father.'

I can't recall hearing the voice of my father's spirit. In life, I felt that he existed in such a stony silence, always staring right through me with his steel gray eyes as if I'd let him down or wasn't doing what he wanted. I think he saw himself in me, and certainly I'm very much my father's daughter. But what was I supposed to do? Did he not forsake me? Or was it the other way around? I've only now begun thinking that perhaps I was the one rejecting him and *that's* why I felt rejected. It's never a one-way street in such matters. And perhaps now, instead of extinguishing him like I've mostly done, I'm resurrecting an old flame?

I've been so worried about Dr Priestly, worried that after her husband's death, things will never be the same again in treatment, worried for myself. Dr Priestly snapped at me that I'm fabricating. But I know she loved her husband very much.

Can I claim to have the capacity to fully love others, really? I mean other than children—because, like Dr Priestly says, I feel safe with children, maybe. But mature love—love in the sense of putting aside my own fears and becoming truly open and receptive, love in the sense of truly taking in a person eye-2-eye.

Am I capable of that? If instead of being suspicious and feeling deprived so much of the time, I could just respond…reach out and gently tug the shimmering threads that tie one human being to another—the threads that illuminate the tapestry of our lives—the ties that bind. I think it must be better to give than to receive, I mean that giving—giving to an Other, giving to Others—can make the giving person feel receptive and full. Maybe that's how to authorize oneself.

Reception Room

I've been spending an awful lot of time lately taking mother for dentures. Get that woman some teeth. What a production but at least it has been surprisingly painless for her, even when we went for oral surgery.

Taking care of her hasn't been easy lately. Last week, one of the many aides I'd brought in quit on the spot because mother pulled a knife on her. The woman said it scared the living daylights out of her. Well sure, but I told her not to be nervous and not to cower, that she was stronger than mother—that mother was basically harmless and to just tell her to behave herself. That went over like a lead balloon so I had to find yet another aide. I'm losing track of how many there've been. It's a merry-go-round of one arriving, another vanishing— because mother doesn't want them. She wants me. But I have to go to work. And I have to live too. The need for care is getting to be 24/7. If only I can get her into Land's End. I keep calling them and she's definitely moving rapidly up the waiting list.

I'm remembering the time I myself had oral surgery. I needed to have a tooth extracted and hadn't realized they'd put me out and finished the procedure when I received my wisdom tooth handed over in a sealed cellophane bag.

I was more than a little elated on medication, I guess so much so that they had me lie down in a room somewhere down the hall. Well, nobody was watching over me and suddenly I jumped up and wandered out of Recovery into the reception room, unaware that blood was drooling out of my mouth down my chin all over the place.

There was a patient sitting on the reception room sofa and he looked so frightened, as if recoiling in horror. I felt so badly. I went over to him and sat right down next to him, trying to comfort and soothe him, help him, I was assuming he was a bit nervous over his impending procedure. I was assuring him everything would be all right.

It was only much later that I realized that I was the Thing that Made him Nervous

See the little baby lying in a manger? <●▬>
Glory hallelujah! Amen! Amen!—American Spiritual

See the little babies?

My head is killing me. Is it a massive resistance to change? So many sessions full of words without my grasping the meaning but really, it doesn't matter. Because answers will emerge and Dr Priestly is my anchor, my one stable thing

I've told her I think of myself on my way to session hysterically upset but when I actually arrive, I shut down. Yes, she says, I seal myself off. I'm holding my baby locked inside. I keep all the good stuff for myself, she says. She tells me that if I were to give birth, the baby from inside would still be mine. But I thought we did this already. I thought I got born already. Didn't I?

Now I've dreamt a surprising dream of giving birth to life amid the stable dung: *I dream my bed is a stable manger. I live with wild animals. Mountain goat, lynx, and wildebeest (wild bees?) are under my head. A little tiger, curled under my shoulder, bites hard into me with its sharp teeth. I try to shift into a more comfortable position. There's someone at the stable doorway—who is it? I think it's Dr Priestly—with Christ-like arms astride—as in Leonardo's drawing—She says to prepare for the reception of more animals that are coming soon*

Dr Priestly's presence at the door is what awakens me. Her presence results in my being bitten. Her presence *is* a bite, a prick, an assault. I awaken to the sensation that she's fiercely extracting the dream from my body. My body is literally contracting as I awaken, as if in the pangs of childbirth

To whom, to what, am I giving birth? What kind of unruly, fierce creation is this little zoo? Is this somehow about Christ in the manger? Christ as the symbol of the self? Yes, a flowering amid the dung—the shit our world is full of? The wild explosive stuff that I am full of…

Dr Priestly is like a Tiger in my path. Is there such a symbol as Christ the Tiger? She seeks what my dreams give: the meat, the love gift—I was right to be afraid. Now I *know* that dreams bite. These little mother-fuckers have teeth. And I know that art—as in the left-handed Leonardo's drawing— is a doorway to frame the angst and suffering of the world.

Tyger! Tyger! burning bright
In the forests of the night

What immortal hand or eye
Could frame thy fearful symmetry?
——The Tyger

Transported

I've been dreaming something fierce, dreaming so many dreams—they're like shooting stars that fall into me out of the night sky:

I dream that at night, radiant dream words are infolded back into the blood from whence they came. I dream that tiny animals arrive in a box with a handwritten note from Dr Priestly—crickets and salamanders and a bird that flies around the room and lands on my head. Then Man and Woman are here with the animals and they tell me about a Bull in storage. There will be a charge for the Bull, a very large charge.

I think this Bull has to come out of storage. This charging Bull, o Toro, a red flag, invincible, electrifying—

●✝▬ Then I have another dream—it wakes me. My heart is pounding:

I cross a railway's path and suddenly see how fast the train is charging in my direction. I'm not sure I can get out of its way fast enough. Then I'm lying down, as if asleep at the switch in my dream, next to the train track and my arm is too close to the Third Rail. All the tracks are curving, overlapping. Smoke is rising from the steel tracks.

I'm sure it's Dr Priestly—in one of her fiery trains of thought. All heat and light, she's electrifying. She shocks me. I shock myself, seeing how magnetized I am by the swerving current. She charges me all right. But I think this dream is speaking to the danger that something deep inside me can explode. And if it's deep enough, I could end up going off the deep end. Dr Priestly directs me to draw this Third Rail dream.

But I can't seem to draw it. All I can think is that Dr Priestly is coming at me— she's a bull, a powerful force, with a heavy charge. And all her training is on a plate before me. I think of the times she has called me good or bad, when she has drawn a line in the sand to show me where not to go. All her training is a kind of sliding contact plate that conducts the world's current—it's a throbbing artery like that Third Rail. And I have to step up to the plate.

{The kingdom of God is within}...

"(Such a) familiar reference should be sufficient to make the psychological position of the Christ symbol quite clear. Christ exemplifies the archetype of the self"—Aion

van der Weyden: The Crucifixion

The resurrection of myself ▓▓ ∏ 回十回 ○ •

I dream I'm at an art exhibit of Angus Christ, Artist. The exhibition begins in the form of a Book. I don't seem to read the words in the Book. Instead, I see red and blue colors bleeding off the pages as the Book tips back into a basin of Blood from whence it came.

Next, I see a doorway to another room. I approach it and see yet another doorway. At that farther doorway stands Christ—Angus Christ—with his left hand nailed to the door frame. I approach him and am now dressed in a long white gown. With my right hand, I release his left hand which he then raises over my right shoulder. He puts his arm around me. I take him in my arms and we dance. He is beautiful. His body is beautiful. When I look down, I see that I am covered in his blood

———

I awakened dazzled by my dream. How beautiful. It's about birth—I said to myself—the spirit in the flesh-and-blood coming to life. And the left hand is the creative spirit.

Christ stands for my self. And Christ resembles Dr Priestly, my dancing partner, my psychoanalyst—a stand-in for—the one who has stood for—my inner self, for restoring me to the heart of my self.

(It would be years later, when I consciously felt painfully aware of my mother's loneliness that I thought: of course, mother is left-handed and I am right-handed. And, in this dream, I with my right hand am the mirror of mother with her left. In this dream, I release her left hand, I lift her from depression, from deadness, and we dance)

Yet, there is more to this dream. It has taken me such a long time to see how rich dreams can be. Every dream is a world…and sometimes what at first seems dark is light, and what seems light proves to include darkness. Nothing is pure.

Behold, the blood of the covenant

For the life of the flesh is in the blood; and I have given it to you upon the altar to make atonement for your souls—Leviticus 17:11

Moses took half the blood and put it in basins and half the blood he dashed against the altar. And he took the book of the covenant and read in earshot of the people and they said: All that the Lord hath spoken, we will do and obey. And Moses took the blood and sprinkled it on the people, saying: Behold, the blood of the covenant.

—Exodus 24: 6-8

Nailed

As I continued to gaze in the mirror of my Angus Christ dream, I saw how *it* was framing *me*. At first, it had struck me as so purely beautiful, portraying me as saving the one (Christ, psychoanalyst, mother) who customarily does the saving. But then I had to ask myself: What was I saving anybody from? from the explosiveness of the bull inside myself? That Bull in storage…

Because surely Angus stood for Angst: Angus, as in Black Angus, cattle, a steak. And the blood in the basin—that little blood curdling exhibit-in-a-bowl—must have come from a bull, or a ram. So then, this was a sacrificial self-portrait: a not-so-charming snapshot of an enraged, artistic bully with a beef, severed from the world artery.

I began pondering the first half of the dream: my body is the Book. Yes, all our bodies are as a Book. Was the dream implying that my not reading the text of the Book meant I was illiterate about myself, about the words, the world, about life? Could I not read the Book of Life? Couldn't I yet do what I was supposed to do in life? Was I still stuck?

The dream portrayed me as stuck at the door, at the entrance to the world, not fully born. Here I'd been struggling to connect with the world and now, this mute dream seemed to suggest that my life was little more than a solipsistic dance inside my head.

Or was it that by dreaming this dream, I was delivering the meat—the love gift—to Dr Priestly? And perhaps I was acknowledging my painful sense of a biological sacrifice (the blood) associated with being female.

Yet one thing was quite clear: my stake in dreaming this dream (or was it its stake in me?) meant that I had to admit that I was the one who'd done the nailing. I was the one who'd nailed my own spirited self, and, for that matter, tried to nail Dr Priestly. Yet, there continued to be more…

Awake o sleeper
and rise from the dead and God shall give you light
—Ephesians 5:14

And that worde was made flesshe—Sancte Jhon 1:14

Door Way

Even though the dream of Angus Christ portrayed me as stuck at the entrance to the world, the dream had doorways—ways to exit this picture, move through this doorframe, to a new, more promising place

So! It is a dream that awakens us to life! Ah, the wallflower is dancing—that's me in the mirror of my dream—dancing an entrancing dance. A wedding dance—I'm wedded to a deeper aspect of myself. To a self who knows suffering; a self who is entering into aliveness

We stand in museums, art exhibitions, at the altar of art—just as in the exhibit of this dream—facing a thousand paintings of the bleeding Christ. The paint bleeds in stillness on the canvas and we call it beautiful. We perceive Art as a doorway to frame the angst and suffering of this world. Art is what flows from our dream life. Our dream life is our life blood—a part of what redeems us—a reparation

Long after this dream, I thought: of course! The doorframe in Dr Priestly's consulting chamber is surrounded by images of Christ and I've been facing them all this time, seeing them—but not consciously taking them in—images of Mary lovingly holding the infant Jesus, images of the crucifixion, the Pieta—I asked Dr Priestly what this doorway wall of paintings meant. She said: Blessings to all who enter here

Perhaps the presence of these sacred paintings on this door way wall is what sparked my dream.

 ∏

Remember Zion?

By the waters of Babylon, there we sat and wept, when we remembered Zion
—Psalm 137

$\mathcal{S}$igmund Freud, speculating even further in **Moses and Monotheism,** wrote that as the Babylonian exile drew to an end:

"...the hope arose among the Jewish people that (Moses) the man they had so callously murdered would return from the realm of the dead and lead his contrite people—and perhaps not only his people—into the land of eternal bliss.....

Then also there is some historical truth in the rebirth of Christ, for he was the resurrected Moses....only transfigured, and as a Son in the place of his Father."

Hippocratic Oath?

Yet—after a dream like this, a glorious dream of dancing with Christ, I ought to be fixed. Why aren't I fixed, Dr Priestly? I mean what more can there be? Am I not blessed in the blood of the Lord? Why am I still consumed in fear and anger? in angst? Tell me

Why aren't I released into the dance of life? Or is it that dreams are just little seeds, seeds that take what feels like an eternity to germinate? How long for transformation? Is there nothing more than this arduous process in life?

And I'm still terrified. Terrified of what? Of death? But what's so frightening about death? All I can think is that the living world will go to dinner and I'll be left behind. No feast for the dead

But now I'm dreaming another dream, a cartoon-like dream, it feels so far away. Is it mine? In the dream, *I'm a river cow—wading in the waters, in the muck.* I've grown from a little snail into a big *Hippo, a monkish, bullish Hippo—and Dr Priestly is a Bird, a river bird, like a heron with stubby wings and a beak that keeps my tongue from wagging.* She has tonsured my tonsils because despite the beauty of my dreams, I'm really not such a beauty sleeping after all. *I look up* to her *and bat my eye lashes.*

Let me go, I lash out. I promise to be good. I'm fixed. Really, I'm altered. I'm transfixed. I want you to say good bye. Good bye bull. But you're silent. Why don't you answer me, Dr Priestly?

I must be talking to myself. Yet, my tongue is a beating heart in your hands. It seems I'm still a child in too many ways, still a patient who seeks healing. I'm frightened of what is yet to come.

So, you cannot leave me—for thou art with me—you cannot fly away and leave me to die here in this river. Or is it a muddy ditch? You cannot leave me not even until the end of time because we've made a pact, you and I. You promised me, you made an oath to deliver me, redeem me. And I too have made an abiding oath, an oath to search out myself

The burning bush

Now Moses—shepherding the flock—came to the mountain of God

where an angel appeared to him as fire in a thorn bush.

Moses beheld: the bush blazed with fire, yet was not consumed.

I must come closer, Moses thought, to see why it is not burned away.

God saw that he approached and called to him from the midst of the bush:
Moses, Moses.

Here am I, Moses answered.

Do not advance, he said. The place where you are standing borders the holy.

—Exodus 3:1-5

A singing tree

The other day I went walking in spring and saw a small cherry tree enfolded in the shape of a tulip.

At first I was utterly dazzled because the tree was chirping its heart out and I thought if only I could sing like that I wouldn't be consumed by grievances and suffering

But then I became aware that there was a bird singing there

Singing in the blossoms, hidden in the branches

How could I be so dumb not to have realized it?

What a slow, slack pupil I am.

Yet I was pleased to perceive that the bush and the bird were one.

The bird was *of* the bush, Dr Priestly said.

And after the fire, a still small voice—1 Kings 19:12

Audition by the book: a dream within a dream

It's before our session and here I am— standing, waiting for Dr Priestly, here in her consulting room, by the book cabinet. Suddenly I hear voices fly up from the printed pages. Am I hallucinating? Is it a miracle of osmosis or am I going off the deep end? Maybe I'm somehow taking to heart what's inside the Books?

I hear the words. The authors' words seem to fly up out of the books the way swallows fly from summer barns, into a musing sky. And just as suddenly, they shrink from sight—inked words, birds, soundless specks that carry wisdom from a realm where we were young again and phantasy was thick. I'm thinking of faraway summers barefoot amid the squash blossoms, and the pond and wild flowers and blueberries and the little foxes and the sea, the meadow down to the sea

I'm looking forward to telling Dr Priestly my new dream. It's a dream as close to the surface as the words flying up from the books. It's a dream within a dream, a dream enveloped in a dream. As in an infinite regress of Russian dolls

In this dream, I recall an older dream about a meadow—what I'd observed there beyond the rim of its hill, just slightly obscured: it's the view I'm seeking —and there it is—the view of my meadow with birds flying above its spinning earth in the early evening light all golden and liquid flowing down to the sea.

And I'm thinking how Dr Priestly has been pressing me more and more to help mother. Mother isn't doing well. And it's so hard meanwhile, while we're waiting to get her into Land's End. Maybe I'm deluding myself—as if wishing her there could make it so. It's just a fantasy—like the fantasy that Dr Priestly would be with me always. I don't mean only in my heart. I mean in real life. Or maybe in the heart *is* real life, the most real of all. And I'm thinking how meanwhile I want to take mother on a trip to that meadow, that meadow in my dream—I want to take her down to the sea. I've begun thinking about airports, and wheelchairs and riding out in the mail boat to all the islands and how my mother would take such pleasure in that.

Behold there ariseth a little cloud out of the sea like a man's hand
—1 Kings 18:44

What the hand dare seize the fire?—The Tyger

Raphael: Christ's Charge to Peter

Renaissance Subtext

I've just returned from an art exhibit of Renaissance tapestries and recalled an old dream of *ice cream cones floating in the sky, like clouds on triangular pillars*. When I dreamt it, I thought it was dumb but now I think it sketched its rudiments like Renaissance cartoons do, on *verso* sides of tapestries—like scant outlines lacking depth or color but signifying what's to come, by turning the page.

Maybe the dream was just a doodle, as if a thing on paper wrapped up in the sleep of itself, patiently enduring the passage of time. But Dr Priestly would help unfurl its message. She would delicately prick its contours and take it up to the light so we could follow the tiny pinhole constellations she'd needled there. So we could better navigate our way through the shifting perspective.

Sometimes I think Dr Priestly has been weaving a kind of tapestry, in bits of color and gold, couching it in a tabernacle frame of pillars, of arms around the (mirror) she's been holding up for me. Holding so I might see aspects of emerging figures, flickering like torches—like my dream's ice cream cone pillars of light.

I know now that when I dreamt that dream, I couldn't yet see that a torch was being held up high at the threshold, the doorway, to love. Yet, just now, at the Renaissance exhibit, I cried at Raphael's study for **Christ's Charge to Peter**. I cried because Raphael's pure love stunned me. He drew a man with hand held high, with fingers like a torch. He drew it as though inscribed in the hand's pure flame, were the words: Come follow me.

It was the hand of Christ—that's what he drew. And he drew it as though it clasped some sort of italic seed. It was as though the hand was blossoming. The very paper itself seemed to have risen—or to be rising-—under that hand—with that seed burrowed in it, under Raphael's hand ❯

Dr Priestly said I cried because I was choking to death on my envy. She said there was no pure love in me. I think I'd begun believing that I'd become so radiant and pure and extraordinarily well-rounded, a true pearl of a girl—that she needed to bring me back to earth by telling me there's no such thing as pure
love. But her words felt like fire, they pierced me, stung me to the core. And having to face the naked truth that I was a million miles from perfect, it felt like I was standing there in my underwear. Then I realized Christ got undressed too.

It shall be a sign upon your hand—Exodus 13:9

The bees invade the text...

I dream of bees biting, gnawing--eating a hole
in my right foot—the place where Christ was crucified.

Bees again…they're everywhere…they're crawling all over my left hand, my
right knuckle they're burrowing their bodies underneath my skin, my knuckles,
my left palm. They're attacking my left palm. Out, get them out. I don't know
how to get them out.

This is a so-help-me-god-awful predicament. Get them out. Help. The bees have
crossed a threshold • the threshold of the night. It must be because I feel stung
by Dr Priestly, that prick who's supposed to be soothing me with lullabies and
hums, not venomously attacking me. Not leaking into my bloodstream. She
crossed a borderline and now I'm bewildered—like a honey bear stumbling into
a swarm of bees. She punctured me with her interventions, stigmatized me with
her interpretations, her so-called pure gold observations that are ruining the
pure gold in me. This isn't fixing me. Instead, I'm forever getting stung by her
observations of how bad I am. She never stops. I can't bear it anymore. I just can't

These dreams are taking over my body, like some fucking horrible inhabitation
◖ These bees are like tics ◖ They won't let go of me. Or I won't let go of them.
This is fucking horrible ◖ I'm trying so hard to be good and follow the right path
and all I do is end up in dreams like these

 It's grisly—they're attacking my left palm. Please help me get rid of them.
I don't know how to get them out • These bloody dreams, this flock of dreams,
this swarm that is of my body

The stigmata, the wounds of Christ

Francis of Assisi spent (too) much time in solitary places
And he went through periods of great uncertainty in his life.

One day, while praying on a mountainside under a tree, he beheld a
vision of a winged creature, a crucified seraph.

It was said that Francis followed in the steps of the Lord. His perfect
fulfillment of the life of Christ was verified by the appearance on his
body of the visible marks of stigmata, the puncture wounds suffered
by Christ during the crucifixion

Leonardo da Vinci: Vitruvian Man

When you make the two into one
You will become children of humanity —Gospel of Thomas 106

Consider the lilies of the field, how they grow —Matthew 6:28

See the pretty girl in that mirror there?

Later, in session, I close my eyes—still exhausted by the dream punctuations. Tormented by bees—how to release myself from them, release them from my hands? I'm beside myself. Dr Priestly presses us forward. I'm stuck. I'm terrified. She has me imagine a projected screen for each hand—one right, one left.

Then, as I'm lying on the couch, the idea enters my head that there's a mirror behind my right shoulder—in the place where Dr Priestly sits. So then, *she* must *be* that mirror.

The mirror projects to another mirror in a far field, a far field that is on the right screen. I hold up my right hand toward the mirror in the far field. And in the distant mirror, I see an imagined real flower. The bee flies out of my right hand, lured by the flower.

Dr Priestly says therefore my hand is a flower.

She says I must be very creative to solve the more difficult task—the left hand. For the life of me, I can't imagine how to help myself. But then somehow I let go into it—and remember something I once read: The observer is the observed. There's no division between them.

Now I know what I have to do. I have to *become* the bee. I close my eyes and with the muscle of my imagination—this being the first time I've ever actively exercised this muscle, the first time I realize there's a creative force in me that I can actively summon—I imagine gently backing my bee body out of my palm and then, I am released. I fly away.

And although Dr Priestly had told me my hand is a flower, it took years for me to take it in, to register this sign upon my hand, held in the mirror, upheld in a mirror of love, for me to see and reflect upon.

𝕭e of good cheere. It is Y, be not afrayed
But when he sawe a mighty winde, he was afrayed.

And as he began to synke, he cryed sayinge: Master, save me.
And immediately Jesus stretched forth his honde
—Matthew 14:27-31

Know that I am with you and will keep you wherever you go
—Genesis 28.15

Wait a minute—I got that backwards

I think a good psychoanalyst has to be a stand-in for the patient's heart. A good psychoanalyst is the one who helps restore the patient to the heart of her self

Dr Priestly has always crouched down with me, no matter what frightening and dark thing I might silently be caught up in. And her crouching down is a kind of standing up for that lost part of me.

I'm feeling very grateful. I feel she is with me. What she has given me is a gift inscribed deep inside me. It's thanks to her I can stand up for myself more often and be a little giving towards others: Know that I am with you and will keep you wherever I go.

Wait a minute—I got that backwards:
Know that I am with you and will keep you wherever **you** go

I guess I have to hand it to her—I've softened a bit. I've even become a little sweet, a bit of a honey. Now and then, I mean. I'm less frightened of others and better able to care more for them than ever before   more for myself and others —like taking care of my mother which I couldn't have done so well without Dr Priestly's encouragement. But still, my heart's kind of cracked, I know. And I really am cold, maybe even a bit like a reptile. I think I still don't have enough sense of equilibrium to fully take in others, to fully stand for myself.

But I'm getting there. I mean I've come to care more for myself. And obviously I couldn't care about anybody else if I didn't care about myself. And the only way *that* happened is that Dr Priestly cared about me and treated me with respect. True respect for who I am.

Climbing Jacob's ladder

Jacob lighted on a certain place and tarried there all night.
He took a stone of that place and put it for his pillow and lay down to sleep.

He dreamed there was a ladder set upon the earth and the top of it reached to heaven; and the angels of God were ascending and descending on it

When he awaked he said: Surely the Lord is in this place and I knew it not.
How dreadful is this place! It must be God's temple. It is the gate to heaven.

—Genesis 28.12-17

The mirror language of our dreams

On the eve of Yom Kippur, I dreamt my left hand is a ladder.
Dr Priestly says the left hand *is* a ladder.

I ask what she means but she remains silent. Maybe it's because the left side
is the heart side. The creative side, the spirited side

I dreamt my left hand has now become a ladder
and a small winged creature, a bee, is flickering
on and off this ladder every time a Tenant
of the Land speaks out in an ancient Hebrew code.

I wonder if the flickering bee is a spirit, a sprite. Like my dream of father coming
back from the dead, with ghosts climbing on the stairs—it's just like the bee
flickering around the ladder. Maybe bees have something to do with death, a
spirit world. I'm reminded that Dr Priestly thinks my bees are birds in disguise.
Maybe she means they symbolize the soul. I myself think my bees are more like
junior hornets with football helmets and shoulder pads.

Maybe this left handed dream speaks—maybe all dreams speak—a mirror
language—like Leonardo's notebooks. Leonardo had a code. Do I have a
code? Can I decode my own code? Can I understand the extraordinary
messages in dreams? These rich and baffling airy nothings—things to be read,
like mirrors, in reverse, perhaps? As in a looking-glass book, from right to left, a
Hebrew code? I think dreams are a turning, a trope to tell the story back to us.

Yes, we dance in halls of mirrors that we call dreams. For surely dreams are the
mirror of the mother. .And father too, Dr Priestly says. And she adds: the bee is
the essence of being. Therefore a ladder is not needed.

Holy, holy, holy

Mother is at Hospital. She's having bad chest pains. It's a Catholic Hospital. Yesterday, when I went to visit, I found her sweetly propped up in bed watching the hospital's private cable station which featured a mass. Mother was singing Holy, holy, holy along with the church choir.

Meanwhile, the Roman Catholic patient in the next bed was watching soap operas on *her* television.

I love my mother. And I'm touched by her singing. And just as soon as she's well enough, we're taking that trip to the meadows and the sea

"In life we have to cross a very narrow bridge.
The most important thing is not to be afraid."

—Rabbi Nachman of Breslov

The Isle of Sky

Mother has recuperated enough for me to be able to wave the wand of my dreams and prepare to take her on the trip I've been thinking about. Dr Priestly helped me uncover the love that has allowed me to do this.

So through airports in wheelchairs, in little planes and big, in cars over tiny bridges—even the pointy little Reach Bridge—I've taken mother all the way to the farthest reaches of the Isle of Sky. It was Dr Priestly who suggested making arrangements for an aide a few hours a day, and having wheelchair assistance when we're in airports. Really helpful ideas

Mother loved the islands for their wild beauty and peacefulness. We took the mail boat to Heron Island and she loved that best. Riding out past tiny islands crowded with pointed fir, out past the magnificent granite coast. We saw baby seals and cormorants and sea ducks. We learned that native bees were being destroyed by migrant bees. Most days, I arranged for helpers to drive mother around to visit gardens and artisans' shops, giving me some time for myself.

And when mother and I traveled around, we sang a lot. That was something we always loved to do together. So now we sang in the car and when we were at sea, we sang everywhere. And despite all the things mother has forgotten and all the things she never remembered, she still knows the lyrics to a million songs.

Oh and did we eat. Chutneys and chowders, grilled rock shrimp and garlic lobster and wild berries and nasturtium and every kind of delicious thing. At meals at the inn, we sat with others—and I was a bridge for mother, helping her join the world. It was very touching to see how delighted she was and also how tentative, and how much help she needed, and how much help she accepted.

And I was happy to help her, happy to be a bridge—just as Dr Priestly has been my bridge —to the world.

This was not an easy trip for us to make. Mother said: thank you for giving me the best two weeks of my life.

"But I am rowing. I am rowing,
though the wind pushes me back
and I know that that island will not be perfect"

—The Awful Rowing Toward God

I'm so lonely

Mother's health has been deteriorating again. She had a fall—a fractured hip. Surgery   She's not eating. She doesn't want to eat. Maybe she's not going to recuperate from this. She's not going to walk again, I don't think. I've been feeling increasingly desperate about what to do. I'm obsessed with getting her into Land's End. She's at the top of the waiting list now but with this lapse in health and with her emotional difficulties, I don't know if we can get her in there.

I took her to a medical specialist Dr Priestly recommended. And mother, even in her condition and at her age, remains vainly flirtatious—so she was livid when I filled in the blanks she'd left out of the picture in describing her health to the doctor. I know she thinks I blabber too much. Recently, she and I had lunch and as I was chattering away, she looked straight past me as she typically did, and said: someone at this table is talking too much.

But it's thrilling that the doctor apparently agrees to say mother is revivable. (Dr Priestly said being revivable would likely be a prerequisite for tenancy at Land's End). And as the doctor was writing up his report, I started worrying again that this place, on which I'd pinned my hopes for her, was a place for well-behaved elderly people. And mother really wasn't what anybody would call well-behaved.

At one point, between the doctor's examination and consulting rooms, I stepped away to get mother's wheelchair and she was left alone—and in that instant, she cried out. From her body, so emaciated, came a raw low moan not exactly like a cat's cry but like something wounded, something guttural, deep in the forest. She cried out three barely audible words: **I'm so lonely**—which made me start crying too because in that instant I felt overwhelmed by her unbearable pain and by all the years of her isolation, I felt overwhelmed knowing what a lost soul she was, overwhelmed knowing that Dr Priestly had put me enough in touch with my own heart to be able to understand the hole in mother's heart.

Despite what he wrote, the doctor said if mother didn't start eating, she'd be dead by fall. And now, within days of having submitted the doctor's report, by what feels like some kind of miracle, we've gotten her into nursing care at Land's End-—and it turns out not everyone there is as well behaved as would be wished. The facility's Christian administrator thoughtfully said mother's coming was meant to be. I'd said as much myself, using what I understood to be the Hebrew word, beshert, meant to be.

To swim in the deep without drowning 〰〰 ※

I visit mother very frequently and I talk to her everyday. Sometimes I sit by her while she sleeps and I think hard thoughts or nothing at all. Sometimes I watch her—her skin so iridescent and her hands so thin. Such a labor of breathing Sometimes I exaggerate my own exhalations, hoping hers might echo this easier way. I try to sit so that at the moment she awakens, she knows that I am here to keep her company

I can't describe what a relief it is that she's at Land's End but still, this is the end, I know. It's coming. In some ways, it's a relief. Yet very sad

I had a dream that *a huge burst of flame—a flame in the shape of a tulip— burned like a burning bush outside my window.* Dr Priestly said she thought the dream was about death. She said the flame is contained, beautiful. I said it felt alien. She asked: alien as the word of God? Yes, I said.

So I wrote a kind of song or psalm, a poem based on the dream. In reading it back to myself, I recalled the times mother read to us when my brother and I were little, in the long-ago glow of antique lamps. She had a way of reading out loud that was naturally beautiful—like her body, her body was beautiful and even now, is beautiful—and when she read, my brother and I laughed our childhood laughs, little squeaks and tiny grunts, practically peeing in our pajamas as we cart-wheeled off the plump sofa onto the bare floor. And from somewhere deep inside, mother's laughter floated through the room.

The poem I wrote—I don't know whether it's for Dr Priestly or mother or both— went like this:

I swim. I am swimming toward you—a torch
aloft in my hand. My fingers are this torch.
Up, up on the waves, I am swimming out
toward the depth of you, the shape of you. Far off,
in my mind's eye, a flame is erupting
to the height of a tree, the shape of a tulip.
Contained, alien, as the word of God

The human soul is the lamp of God

Mother died on June 27. I buried her next to where I myself will most likely be buried. Whither thou goest, I will go, whither thou diest, I will die—and there will I be buried   Well, maybe. Maybe I'll be buried there too.

The night of the burial I was comforted by the thought that this was her first night in the earth, buried in the earth—next to the pines, under the stars, out there in the meadow. But the next night, there was a terrible thunderstorm and I imagined the pouring rain and muddied earth leaking into her coffin, drizzling over her face and body. And I grew terribly upset thinking of the decaying process of my mother's body, of her face like wax, that it would be eaten away. The idea of the muddied decay was unbearable   It was making me sick.

Dr Priestly told me I was making a statue of my mother's body. She said I felt like my mother's body was my body. She said I felt like it was my body in there and what she said helped me because I don't suppose I've ever been quite certain where my mother's body or anybody leaves off and I begin.

The next night, I listened to Dawn Upshaw's recording of *Sing for Your Supper.* I sobbed thinking mother would never again hear a Rodgers & Hart song, she'd never hear it and we'd never sing it. But it was consoling to remember that mother's love of music was in me and that, wherever I go, I'll carry it with me.

Actually, the last words I heard mother speak—she sang them—were the lyrics from Irving Berlin's *Blue Skies.' Blue days all of them gone, nothing but blue skies from now on.'* She was gazing right past me, as usual, but looking up, out into the sky—and I knew this was the end. When I told Dr Priestly about mother's song, she said that it had been a gift. It was embracing death.

Of course I was so happy that I'd taken mother on that trip to the Isle of Sky. I was so happy I'd taken care of my mother these past years and that I could do the right thing and that I wanted to give her pleasure and be a good daughter.

So now I'm an orphan in the world, as my mother had been. And now, right now, it's so comforting to burn a mourner's candle for seven days. The words prayed over the lighting of this candle are: The human soul is the lamp of God.

For where your treasure is, there will your heart be also—Mathew 6:21

The kingdom that is the self, the pearl of great price; the treasure buried in the field
—adapted from Aion

... ●

Treasured Chest

Oddly enough after so many years, I've just now recalled the antique travel trunk mother got when I was four—we called it a Treasure Chest and it was placed in my room, to be used as my toy chest. It had sharp-edged brass fittings, loose hinges and a very heavy lid, and it could easily have cut into my little head, my neck, whenever I opened it up and leaned into it to pull out my playthings.

That Treasure Chest has been stowed away under a heap of cushions in my attic for all these years. Isn't it interesting that even though I rarely saved most things and had totally forgotten about *this* thing, I had kept it, stashed away...
A storage chest in storage

It was my own treasured chest, my bosom, my heart—with all its treasures buried there in that place that had been so cut off.

Sometimes when I can't think anymore or when somehow I'm stuck, I just lay my head down on my desk, with my tongue hanging out somewhat in the manner of a small animal panting as it lays in the meadow on a hot summer's day. And it's good, Dr Priestly says, because there are so many things that cannot be solved with one's head.   But the body knows, and the dreams that are of the body

As when I've had to endure a painfully long medical procedure, I go, as Dr Priestly taught me, I go in my imagination, to my meadow—to the deep core of that place where the night sky rises up before the world. And the sky is full of billions of stars and then it's morning in the world where the sea stretches out beyond the beautiful fields filled with lilies and little foxes and all the sounds of the earth coming to life, and the voices of those dearest to me

Evening Seders

In every generation we celebrate Passover. As it is said (in Exodus 12:14):

And this day shall be unto you for a memorial; and you shall keep it a feast to the Lord throughout your generations.

During the Passover meal—the Seder—during the eons of evening Seders, we recline on the couch and ponder the meaning of the Exodus, the deliverance of the children from bondage, the story of how we were slaves unto Pharaoh in Egypt and how, with a mighty hand, God brought us forth out of the house of bondage, out of the land of affliction, across the Sea.

We learn what going forth, dreaming, feasting in the world's wilderness mean. We learn to cherish the blessing of life—what it means to be alive. We thank God for having enabled us to reach this holiday season. We open the Passover book—the Hagaddah—and read with our children so they might learn the order of things, our place in the world order, how the pieces of the world are bound together.

Our children ask: Why is this night different from all other nights?

And parenthetically, as we ponder such questions, year in and year out, we learn what affliction and struggle and birth and morality mean. And love also. We learn what love means

Evening Sessions

I've begun thinking that all our evening sessions have been like evening Seders, led by my Christian psychoanalyst

Of course, it's not as though Seders are foreign to Christians
The Last Supper, after all, was a Passover Seder—a Seder led by one of the world's most extraordinary rabbis—Jesus of Nazareth

What made these nights so special was the way we were together, catching all those dreams—catching them like fish. An entire school of fish, darting in the sea. It was a world to be discovered, to be borne. Every dream is a world, as Dr Priestly has said.

Her chamber has grown dimmer now. But of course, I look back, through the pinhole camera of memory, into that world of light and love, to all those evenings together, with me lying on the couch, over the years, learning, as best I could, to take the measure of my days.

In the end, face-to-face with her, I knew it hadn't been a picnic. But it was a feast. I looked into her eyes, her face so warm, so open. Yes, she was an open book. I knew it now, as she once years ago had told me. And then, I remember at the end, she took me by the hand—or perhaps it was I who took her hand—and we went out together through the double doors of her consulting room. The double doors that gave a wide enough berth for the two of us to go our separate ways in the world

Rest in Peace

It has been a year since my mother died. And the time has come for the unveiling of her gravestone. I dreamt a dream a few days before the occasion.

Unveiled

I dream of a bat that is flying around holding a small black square of veil. I'm afraid it will get into my hair. I sit, with my knees raised. The earth is hard. Dr Priestly says: afraid and alone.

I feel angry and depressed at the finality of death. Yet, I know this is a good dream. Clear and straightforward, I sit on a fleshy geography, the hard stone of reality. I suppose there's the innuendo that I'm casting my mother as an old bat out of hell, that she had bats in her belfry, she was a little nuts. And maybe I'm acknowledging that we can all be blind as bats sometimes, when we're not willing to see, eye-to-eye, when we forget how small we are.

Despite all the negative things about my mother, still there was a basic goodness in her. Goodness that didn't develop enough. Goodness that was too fleeting. But whatever I got, it came from my mother. And Dr Priestly helped me develop it. Of course, none of this is to say that I didn't receive many things from my father. I certainly did.

The dream's veil clearly speaks to the unveiling of my mother's gravestone. And perhaps, the dream's veil is to cover my head in the face of something bigger than I.

Afraid and alone, the dream says. Yes, there are many moments when I'm afraid. I'm trying to remain undeterred by fear. And alone—I think of what Dr Priestly told me: to be alone is a gift, the precious gift of individuality.

Now Yahweh planted a garden in Eden, eastward, settled there the man he formed. From the land Yahweh grew all trees lovely to look upon, good to eat from; the tree of life was there in the garden, and the tree of knowing good and bad   —Genesis 2:8–9 (The Book of J)

Even soo evry good tree bryngethe forthe good frute…wherefore by their frutes ye shall knowe them.   —Matthew 7:17, 20

He was nailed to a tree (and) he became a fruit of the knowledge of the Father. It did not, however, cause destruction because it was eaten, but to those who ate it, it gave (cause) to become glad in the discovery, and he discovered them in himself, and they discovered him in themselves.
          —The Gospel of Truth 18:24–29, NHL

The fruit of the tree of our life

I dream that a beautiful tree of life springs up right in front of a pine tree. It seems almost to have been grafted from that pine, as though from the healing properties of its sap—out of the resin of its old wood. Both trees are filled with fruit, red fruit.

I don't know whether one is a tree of our life and the other a tree of knowing good and bad. Or whether both are both? I think my two trees are mother and offspring, and also Dr Priestly and myself. And the resin is the resonance and the sap is the honey, the pure healing honey that seeps directly into the bloodstream. The sap courses through the trees just as the blood courses through our veins. And I think both these trees are aspects of myself

Mostly, I can see that life is the fruit of our own doing.

I can see now that I've come to life and in coming to life, I'm coming to better know myself, my reaches and limits. I've come to know good and bad. And I've come to appreciate who I am and what I have. And I'm coming to know and care about others, coming to know that human feeling is no foreign song.

THE END

Sources

Armstrong, Karen. *In the Beginning: A New Interpretation of Genesis,* Knopf, 1996
Beckett, Samuel. *Endgame,* Grove Press, 1958
Blake, William. *The Tyger,* from *Songs of Experience,* 1794
Bloom, Harold; and Rosenberg, David, Transl. *The Book of J,* Grove Weidenfeld, 1990
Bloom, Harold. *Jesus and Yahweh The Names Divine,* Riverhead Books, 2003
Bloom, Harold. *Where Shall Wisdom Be Found?,* Riverhead Books, 2004
Campbell, Joseph. *The Power of Myth,* Doubleday, 1988
Cantor, Norman. *The History of the Middle Ages,* HarperCollins, 1963
Field, Eugene. *Wynken, Blynken and Nod (Dutch Lullaby),* 1889
Freud, Sigmund. *Moses and Monotheism,* Random House, 1939, 1967
Herford, R. Travers. *Sayings of the Fathers (Pirke Aboth)* Jewish Institute of Religion 1945
Jung, Carl. *Aion: Researches into the Phenomenology of the Self,* Princeton University Press, 1959
Jung, Carl. *Symbols of Transformation,* Princeton University Press, 1956
Jung, Carl. *Psychology and Religion,* Yale University Press, 1966
Nachman of Breslov,Rabbi. *Likutey Moharan II, Lesson 48,* Breslov Rsearch Institute, 1999
Pagels, Elaine. *Beyond Belief: The Secret Gospel of Thomas,* Random House, 2003
Pagels, Elaine. *The Gnostic Gospels,* Random House, 1979
Robinson, Marilynne. *Gilead,* Picador, 2004
Sexton, Anne. *The Awful Rowing Toward God,* Houghton Mifflin Company, 1975
The Gospel of Thomas, from *The Complete Gospels: Annotated Scholars Version* 3rd Edition,
      Robert J. Miller, Polebridge Press, 1992,1994
The Gospel of Truth, from *The Nag Hammadi Library,* James M. Robinson, Editor, HarperCollins, 1990
The Hagaddah: Instructions for the Passover Seder, Nathan Goldberg, Ktav, 1993
The Holy Bible, King James Version, New American Library, 1974
The Living Torah, Aryeh Kaplan, Transl, Maznaim, 1981
The New Testament, William Tyndale, Transl, Worms Edition1526, British Library. 2000
The Pentateuch & Haftorahs, J.H. Hertz, Editor, *Soncino Press,* 1960
The Tanakh, Jewish Publication Society, 1985

Photo/Art Credits

Duccio di Buoninsegna, *The Calling of the Apostles Peter and Andrew,* 1308/1311, tempera on panel.
      Samuel H. Kress Collection, Image courtesy of the Board of Trustees, National Gallery of Art,
      Washington, DC
Leonardo da Vinci. *Vitruvian Man,* ca 1492, drawing. Reprinted with permission of Scala/Art Resource, NY
Raphael, *Christ's Charge to Peter,* ca 1514. Reprinted with permission of The Royal Collection © 2007
      Her Majesty Queen Elizabeth II
Rogier van der Weyden, *The Crucifixion,* ca 1450-55, Right panel, oil and gold. Reprinted with
      permission of The Philadelphia Museum of Art, Philadelphia, PA/Art Resource, NY

In memory of my mother, who didn't have the chance
to become the person she was meant to be.

Acknowledgements

More than once, Dr Priestly said that she and I might one day write a
book together. In a sense, this is that book, that book of ours—even
though, despite my best intentions, what I've attributed to her and what
she actually said and did—may not always be one and the same.

I wish to express my gratitude for the love and devotion of my husband
Steven and my son Noah.

Also, for their generous insights, counsel, and aid in creating this book,
I am indebted to Bernard Ehrenberg, Linda Karshan, Linda Loewenthal,
Austin Metze, Sheila Ronsen, and Joelle Shefts.

And to my brother, whom I dearly love